D1507124

Remembering | CHARLES KURALT

Ralph Grizzle

Remembering
CHARLES KURALT

HUGH MORTON

The
Globe
Pequot
Press

Guilford, Connecticut

ISBN 0-7627-1184-1

Library of Congress Card Number 00-101284

Manufactured in the United States of America

FIRST GLOBE PEQUOT EDITION/FIRST PRINTING

Design by Marjorie Grizzle

Companion web site for this book
www.rememberingcharleskuralt.com

The publishers have generously given
permission to use extended quotations from
the following copyrighted works.

A Life On The Road
Copyright © 1990 by Charles Kuralt
Reprinted by permission of Putnam Berkley,
a division of Penguin Putnam

North Carolina Is My Home
Copyright © 1998 by Charles Kuralt
Reprinted by permission of
The Globe Pequot Press, Guilford, CT
www.globe-pequot.com

Academy of Achievement excerpts reprinted
with permission of The Academy of Achievement
www.achievement.org

For Marjorie, Britton, Alex,
mom and dad.

Acknowledgments

——

PUTTING TOGETHER *REMEMBERING CHARLES KURALT* was a lot like an old-fashioned barn raising. That is to say I did not have to go far to find talented people to pitch in. They were all just around the corner or just down the road. In some cases, they were even closer. My wife Marjorie brought to the task not only her love, patience and unwavering support but also her wonderful book design and production skills, all while shouldering more than her share of raising our two toddlers.

While his native home is Australia, Trent Bouts is now a neighbor living just a few blocks away. He and Betty Work, from Greensboro, marshalled their editorial talents to finesse the words and phrases—the building blocks—of this book. A former colleague, Sarah Lindsay, made sure those words and phrases were consistent with our style book. When Sarah is not proofreading text during her day job for a Greensboro publishing company, she's writing award-winning poetry.

A couple of hours north on the Blue Ridge Parkway, Hugh Morton kept the U.S. Postal Service busy delivering his photographs of Kuralt from Linville, North Carolina, to Asheville. The steward of one of the country's most beautiful natural areas, Grandfather Mountain, Hugh was among Kuralt's best friends.

Edwin M. Yoder Jr. artfully remembered his old friend in the foreword; Jay Anning, my wife's uncle, provided a guiding hand over the book's design; Mary Ellis and Bernie Mann, of North Carolina's *Our State* magazine, supported the concept of this book from the start and continue to do so; Vann Boyd and Betsy Viator, both good friends, played the roles of critics.

Others chipped in: UNC Archivist Jill Snider brought order to the near 60,000 items in the Charles Kuralt Collection—vital to this book; the family of Charles Kuralt generously permitted the use of many of the letters and photographs inside these pages; the University of North Carolina dusted off old issues of the college annual *Yackety Yak* and allowed use of photos from Kuralt's days at UNC; and the contributors to the Charles Kuralt Collection made possible the funding of the oral histories that gave structure to *Remembering Charles Kuralt*. And, of course, the people who had the good fortune to know Kuralt graciously shared their memories of an old friend.

Charles Kuralt would have admired the spirit of community that went into the making of this book. I am ever grateful. Thank you to all.

Ralph Grizzle
March 2000
Asheville, North Carolina

It really is rewarding to keep your eyes open and permit yourself to be detoured. I understand that people want to have as many experiences as they can crowd into whatever time they have. It's the condensation of time. We all have so little of it.

—Charles Kuralt
1994 interview

Contents

Foreword

THOMAS A. EDISON HAD IT WRONG. Genius, he said, is "1 percent inspiration and 99 percent perspiration." That may be true of tinkerers and inventors. But in the world of creativity, written and verbal, it is nonsense. And nothing proves it like the life and career of Charles Bishop Kuralt.

I had the good fortune to see Charlie's genius when it was still partially concealed in the chrysalis of youth. When we met for the first time in the offices of *The Daily Tar Heel* in Chapel Hill one day in 1953, we both were college sophomores. At that age one is still too raw—I was, anyway—to see far beyond the immediate evidence. But in his case the signs of what was to come were unusually obvious.

Our mutual friend, the witty and learned manager of Graham Memorial, Jimmy Wallace, had already nicknamed Charlie "Mellifluous," a label implying a flow of words vaguely specious. Jimmy was wrong, and so were all those who failed to detect something quite unusual. I knew Charlie then as a friend. He was that genial and slightly pudgy young man with the splendidly resonant voice who had been anointed Rolfe Neill's successor as editor of the *Tar Heel*. He still faced an election, but that proved to be a formality, as expected, especially after Charlie took the pledge before the University Party caucus that the *Tar Heel* would mute its scolding of what we called "big time" (commercialized) athletics. It did no such thing, of course, but the scolding became far more urbane and good humored at Charlie's hands.

As his associate editors, Louis Kraar and I could see that Charlie had a special touch at the typewriter. His portable, as I recall, wore a reminder: "People don't always have to clobber each other." His mentors and models were journalists like Eric Sevareid and E. B. White, who mused more than they shouted. Their influence came through in small but telling touches. When Fred Weaver, the elegant and friendly dean of students, issued a sudden decree suspending all consumption of alcohol in fraternity houses, Charlie was ready. With a wry glance across the Atlantic, he wrote perhaps the only three-word editorial ever to grace our garrulous editorial columns. "Pierre, meet Fred," it said in its entirety, an allusion to the milk-drinking campaign then being waged, to great notoriety, by the French prime minister, Pierre Mendes-France. Mendes-France sought to wean French workingmen from their murderous daily wine-bibbing: "Never more than a single liter of wine a day" was the motto. I have forgotten the outcome of Fred Weaver's campaign, and Pierre's too, for that matter. I haven't forgotten that little squib of an editorial. It was a trademark Kuralt product.

Now, let's fast forward some 15 years. It is now 1970, or thereabouts, and Charlie, well past his apprentice days as a scriptwriter for the Douglas Edwards news program on CBS and stints here and abroad of reporting, had found the form that would forever carry his patent: the "On the Road" series. He toured the country in a van with a cameraman looking for those vignettes of American life that busier, more conventional reporters tended to miss. It might be something as slight as boys rolling happily in autumn leaves in a small New England town, or the dedication of a craftsman who had been hand-making brick in North Carolina for many decades: tremendous trifles, as G. K. Chesterton might have called them. The discovery of the form seems to have been something of an accident. Walter Cronkite has confessed that he was a bit skeptical at first. But the form was an instant success because it engaged all of Charlie's special strengths: an ingenious ability to sound an "ordinary" scene with the radar of his own character and to translate the returning signals into rich and fetching whimsy. Amateurs at writing sometimes patronize whimsy—but only because they haven't tried it. What seems so effortless demands the surest touch, whether one thinks of E. B. White's best *New Yorker* "casuals" or their visual equivalent in Kuralt's "On The Road" pieces.

Under close analysis—which as Wordsworth said of over-examined poetry, would "murder to dissect"—we would see that the key to what came out was what went in. Charlie's pieces, whether written or televised, were in a special way reflections of his personal and God-given slant on the world. Never has the French adage been truer: *Le style, c'est l'homme lui-meme;* the style is the man himself. Charlie as I knew him for more than 40 years was an enjoying man, touched by wanderlust and longing for experience, with the patience to probe until he penetrated beyond the obvious and touched that indwelling strain of uniqueness that we like to think is intrinsic in all of us—if only we had Kuralts to find it. The savor of his writing, brief or at length, stemmed from

Charlie's capacity to define the core and essence of what he saw, and never at second hand. "Make it new," Ezra Pound advised poets. "See it new" might have been Charlie's watchword, not that he needed to be told.

And he did have words to go with the pictures. Seeing and writing were, for him, opposite sides of the same coin. The tone, the choice of words, was always exact and often enchanting. Which is, incidentally, why most of the imitators falter. I remember once when Charlie was talking about his boyhood in eastern North Carolina, when everybody had a stick horse to ride. "And then there was my friend Charles," he said, a boy from a wealthy family, "who had a horse for a horse." The same wit that I had known for many decades was at play on a November evening in 1994, when the National Press Club in Washington gave Charlie its coveted Fourth Estate Award. Four friends, of whom I was one, had been brought in to reminisce. I said that Charlie's view of life was so benevolent that had he stumbled into Shakespeare's "Macbeth," he probably would have done an "On The Road" piece about the "weird sisters," the witches, and found something to like about them. Charlie, who knew my streak of pedantry from way back, retorted: "Yoder still needs an editor." Calvin Trillin, another of the speakers, said his piece; and it was witty and funny. Could Charlie top it? He could. Trillin, he said, had once been a real journalist (the Kuralt pose that evening was that of the five speakers he was the only authentic journalist) but now had become a "swell," nearly as well known as, say, Margaret Truman, whose name appeared with his on a list of well-known Americans. "He writes poetry for *The Nation*," Charlie said drily. He paused. "It is minor poetry."

Perhaps what I am talking about—and surely it will emerge in the valuable and vivid reminiscences of friends and colleagues that Ralph Grizzle has put together here—is a point that Edison missed, at least when it comes to art and craft. Occasionally, and too rarely, there comes among us a voice destined from the cradle to practice alchemy on our common experience. What may seem ordinary, base metal, even leaden, becomes at his touch transformed so that it glimmers with the polish of pure gold. It is of course a form of magic, and Charles Bishop Kuralt was a magician.

Edwin M. Yoder Jr.
March 2000

Preface

——

A T HIS DEATH ON JULY 4, 1997, Charles Kuralt left behind
an abundance of letters, scripts, tapes, photographs
and other mementos that speak to a life fully lived.
Most of the material found a home at the University of North
Carolina at Chapel Hill. It was an obvious and appropriate
choice. Kuralt said he spent some of the "finer, freer, more
stimulating" years of his life on the UNC campus, and it was
the place where he asked, in his final days, to be buried.

The Charles Kuralt Collection is packed away for preser-
vation purposes in acid-free folders and boxes. Open to
researchers, it is a vast collection, encompassing more than
60,000 items. And it continues to grow, as the Kuralt family
and others donate even more memorabilia to the university's
Manuscripts Department. Poring through the boxes of fan
mail, it becomes clear that Kuralt left an indelible impression
on the people who watched him on television, people who
felt they knew him personally.

But it is hard to capture the life of Charles Kuralt through memorabilia alone. We knew him best through the people and the voices he shared with us along the way, and it seems fitting that those voices from his past should be a part of the way we remember him. So in the spring of 1998, the Kuralt Collection archivists and a group of fund-raisers elected to undertake an oral history that would preserve on tape the memories and impressions—the voices—of Charles Kuralt's friends, family and colleagues as part of his enduring life story.

As a contributing editor to North Carolina's *Our State* magazine, I knew about the oral history project and earnestly wanted to be part of it. I had been lucky enough to interview Charles Kuralt, in 1994, and was enthralled by this remarkable man. I volunteered for the job and, partly because of that time I had spent with Kuralt, they gave it to me.

A N ORAL HISTORY BEGINS with the tracking down of people. There were the obvious candidates—Wallace Kuralt, Charles' brother, who lives in Chapel Hill; friends in Charlotte, where Kuralt attended junior and senior high school and worked for the *Charlotte News*, one of the city's two daily papers in his day; and colleagues at CBS in New York.

To find others whose lives had intersected with Kuralt's, I reread his six books and sought out some of the people he interviewed on television. I visited with as many people as I could and talked by phone with those too far away or otherwise difficult to reach.

In the end, I talked with nearly 100 people, collecting more than 60 hours of interviews and transcribing 1,200 pages of notes. The tapes and transcripts form the basis of this book.

It is important to note that this is not a biography, but a collection of narratives and anecdotes intended to celebrate—and provide some insights into—the life of Charles Kuralt.

The spirit of *Remembering Charles Kuralt* is best summed up by a line from British playwright J.M. Barrie, who said in 1922: "God gave us memory so that we might have roses in December." Kuralt presented us with beautiful stories and beautiful people—roses, to help us remember.

My father backed the Chevrolet out of its place in the hay barn next to the farm cart and helped my mother into the front seat on the afternoon of September 9, 1934. ... I was born the next morning with rambling in my blood and fifty miles already under my belt.

—Charles Kuralt,
A Life on the Road

Where The Road Began

(Eastern North Carolina, 1934–44)

P OPULAR HISTORY WILL TELL YOU THAT Charles Bishop Kuralt was born in Wilmington, North Carolina. He _was_ born there, as the records indicate, but only because it had a hospital. At the time of his birth on September 10, 1934, Kuralt's parents were living with his maternal grandparents on their 100-acre tobacco farm in Onslow County. Worried about possible complications from delivering the baby at home, Wallace Kuralt drove his young wife Ina to James Walker Memorial Hospital, a little more than an hour south. After the birth, the family immediately returned to the farm.

The distinction between where Kuralt was born and where he was raised is important. He grew up not as a city-dweller but as a farm boy who later acquired a thin veneer of city sophistication. Named for his paternal uncle, Carl (Norse for "a man of the common people"), Kuralt would remain forever connected to his rural roots.

Cradled in his mother's arms, Charles Kuralt was born in the port city of Wilmington but raised on the same Onslow County farm as was his mother. Being raised on a farm accounted for Kuralt's neighborly mien and ambling Southern disposition. On television, he sometimes appeared as though he were leaning on a fencepost, dispensing rural wisdom to devoted viewers.

The farmhouse where Kuralt spent much of his childhood had no electricity. In winter, wood stoves and fireplaces worked to heat the high-ceilinged rooms. There was no indoor plumbing. On the porch, a pump with a long cast-iron handle delivered drinking water. A gourd on a nearby nail served as a drinking dipper. There was a well in the side yard, with a bucket for watering the stock.

In later years, Kuralt would credit his grandmother, Rena Bishop, with developing his love of words and rhythm of language.

Life was full of simple pleasures. Kuralt spent his days flying kites of newspaper held rigid by flour paste, making slingshots from dogwood branches, and tickling Venus flytraps shut with a piece of straw. "I knew how to turn a double page of *The News & Observer* into a kite held together by flour paste," Kuralt would later write, "and I knew how to fly it on a length of tobacco twine above the barn, above the fields, high enough, as I imagined, that God could read the headlines if He wished."

Evenings, his grandmother, Rena Bishop, stoked a fire to warm well water, which she poured into an old galvanized tub to wash the dust from her grandson.

After supper, his grandfather spun long yarns, and the youngster sat spellbound by his voice. On the front porch of their two-story farmhouse, Kuralt often curled up beside his grandmother on the swing and listened as she read to him from the travel books of Richard Halliburton, the short stories of O. Henry and the poems of Kipling and Poe. Her

reading fueled his love of words and sensitivity to the rhythm of language. It was from her that he first heard words like "pyramid," "igloo" and "Taj Mahal."

Kuralt slept upstairs in a feather bed. The wind rushing through the Sycamores often broke his slumber, forcing him to lay awake. Staring up at the high lath on the ceiling, he wandered through waking dreams of the stories his grandmother had read to him.

His father worked in the Springfield, Massachusetts, Armory, manufacturing rifles for the Army. But Wallace Kuralt wanted more from life, and at age 19 he headed south to Chapel Hill to pursue a degree in business. Graduating at the depth of the Depression, he eventually landed work in social services —because he could type.

NORTH CAROLINA COLLECTION,
UNC LIBRARY AT CHAPEL HILL

B EING DELIVERED into the Great Depression provided the boy with lessons of hardship. His parents, both graduates, emerged from the university into a world of dim career prospects.

A native of Springfield, Massachusetts, Wallace Hamilton Kuralt graduated from UNC in 1931 with a Phi Beta Kappa key and a degree in commerce, but he found little sustaining work. Making a living often meant chasing one. The young man ventured all the way to Charleston, West Virginia, finding a job in the advertising division of the Kroger Grocery Co.

He left behind his sweetheart, Ina Bishop, a home economics teacher in Hillsborough, North Carolina. The two had met on an eight-week, cross-country trip sponsored by UNC. Wallace noticed the attractive young schoolteacher early in the trip, but it took him several days to muster the courage to approach her. He finally broke the ice by offering her a taste of a new soft drink. In later years, they joked they had Dr. Pepper to thank for bringing them together.

W ALLACE LASTED ONLY a few months in the hills of West Virginia, returning to North Carolina to marry Ina shortly before Christmas, 1931. The newlyweds made the Bishops' tobacco farm their first home. There, Wallace tried his hand raising "truck" crops such as snap beans and cucumbers, but the cost of trucking the vegetables to market proved too great. He also tried his hand at raising grapes, but the sandy Onslow County soil was ill-suited to the vines. Even had he succeeded, there was no market for grapes, according to Horace Gurganus, a relative who worked with Wallace.

A graduate of East Carolina Teachers College, Ina Bishop was teaching home economics in Hillsborough, North Carolina, when in 1930 she signed up for a cross-country trip sponsored by UNC. On that trip, she met Wallace Kuralt.
EAST CAROLINA UNIVERSITY

To eke out a living, Wallace turned to a variety of jobs, including painting Coca-Cola signs on barns and creosoting telephone poles. He "topped" tobacco for $1.50 a day and even tried to make a go of operating a farm supply store in nearby Jacksonville.

In 1933, his fortunes changed. The Federal Emergency Relief Administration posted a job for a "social case worker"

Young Charles with his father.

for Onslow County, one of the few specialties in demand among millions of unemployed. Kuralt later would say his father landed the job "because he could type." No matter. After a few months, Wallace won a promotion to county director of rural rehabilitation, and soon after his son was born he gained an even bigger promotion, to social services case supervisor for Robeson County, 100 miles away.

THE KURALTS PACKED THEIR BAGS and moved to Lumberton, the county seat, and Wallace quickly climbed the ranks to become director of social services for a seven-county district in eastern North Carolina.

It was a time of frequent relocation, but also of growing career stability. Two years into the job, Wallace decided to make social work a lifelong career and in the fall of 1937, began attending the University of North Carolina's Graduate School of Social Work at Chapel Hill. To support the family, Ina found work in Stedman, a hamlet east of Fayetteville. Barely 2 years old, Charles seemed to be following the same destiny as his forebears, shipping from one town to another.

> *I come from wandering tribes, Norse and Celtic on my mother's side it seems, nomad Bavarians on my father's, ancestors become Scots-Irish and Slovenian by the time of their migration to America. As far as I could tell, none of them ever stayed anywhere for long.*
>
> —Charles Kuralt, *A Life on the Road*

IN STEDMAN, the Kuralts rented three rooms in an unpainted house on Euclid Street. On trips back to the farm, Charles boasted that the apartment had indoor plumbing.

From his bedroom window, Charles could see the brick building where his mother taught home economics. On

Sunday afternoons, he looked out his bedroom window to watch his father walking across the street, with a black suitcase in hand, and sticking out his thumb, to catch a ride to Chapel Hill for a week of classes in social work. It was a routine that lasted a year, hitching to Chapel Hill on Sundays and returning home, sometimes by bus or train, after the end of Friday classes. In a 1994 letter, Kuralt recalled those early days when his father returned home for the weekend.

Dear Papa,

I was just sitting here in the office thinking about your birthday tomorrow and the inadequacy of any birthday present to express my love for you. No wool shirt or bathrobe or box of cigars could come close to doing it. Nothing I could ever give you could equal what you have given me. I remember the excitement I felt in Stedman on weekends when you came home from Chapel Hill because I knew you'd find time to play with me. I remember your teaching me to throw and catch a baseball in the yard of the apartment house in Washington, and your patience with me when I missed an easy catch. You were always willing to "tame a mosquito" with a puff of cigar smoke, and I was always delighted at the joke. You took me fishing on the river. I remember the thrill of being out there in the boat with you, sure that we'd catch fish because you knew how. I was certain of your competence in everything—fishing, typing, sign painting, carpentry—and knew I'd never be as able. And I was right. But you made me want to be, which is almost the same.

When I asked some childish question about science, you brought me home a cardboard microscope; when I despaired at ever getting good at mumblety-peg, you taught me a few good tricks the other boys couldn't do, and gave me a jackknife of my own in the bargain. Remember the BB gun? It was a Red Ryder single shot model, and I was exceedingly proud of it—but I had to learn the multiplication table before I could take it out of the house. There was the red Elgin bike you gave me when I was five, and the new car when I was nineteen. My pleasure in all these gifts was immeasurably greater because they came from you.

But of course the greatest gift was our time together. I am thinking of all those nights when you drove me to Griffith Park so I could broadcast baseball games, and then waited until the ninth inning and drove back to pick me up. I was always eager to hear you say I had done a good job on the air. The feeling of driving home with you in, as I thought then, manly camaraderie, was a very fine feeling; you must have had all sorts of concerns of your own, but mine were the only ones you ever talked to me about. You gave me great confidence. I didn't know it then, but you were teaching me how to be a father, and how to be a good man. I can never be as good a father or as good a man as you were, and are.

I realize that most of my attitudes and beliefs came from you and mother, including some basic ones that animate me to this day. I sometimes find myself eagerly articulating an idea which, when I stop to think about it, I heard you express with feeling long ago.

So I am my father's son. I hope I have passed along something of you to [daughters] Lisa and Susan, and that they will pass that essence of you on to their children, and so on down the generations. And I know that [brother] Wallace and [sister} Catherine share the same hope in their own lives. Thank you, Papa. Happy birthday. With all my love, Charles

Summertimes and holidays, we often returned to my mother's home in the corner of Onslow County that longtime residents still refer to as "Southwest." I remember every detail of life there on the 100-acre tobacco farm that seemed to me the authentic center of the world. I remember my grandfather, John Bishop, his white mustaches tobacco-stained, clad in overalls. I was in awe of him. He could do anything. I am acquainted with city people who think of country people as backward and uneducated. I knew better than that before I was 6 years old.

—Charles Kuralt, pictured with his grandfather John Bishop.

A FTER A YEAR OF GRADUATE STUDY, Wallace found work as a field representative for the North Carolina Welfare Board. The job required another move, to Salisbury, where the family lived in a brick house overlooking the highway. There, Kuralt gained a sibling when Ina gave birth to a second son, Wallace Jr.

The family stayed in Piedmont North Carolina only a short while before relocating to the Welfare Board's eastern headquarters in Washington, an hour's drive from the Bishops' tobacco farm. His father's new job gave 4-year-old Charles a taste of being on the road, as he often accompanied "Papa" to local welfare offices in the county seats of eastern North Carolina. Riding along blacktop roads to places like New Bern, Swan Quarter, Harkers Island and Edenton, Wallace filled the miles and his young son's mind with tales of North Carolina history and local lore.

Afternoons, they stopped to fish in creeks turned black by the tannin of cypress trees. At country stores and outside the county courthouses where the welfare offices were located, father and son stopped to listen to old men trade stories. Kuralt later said that traveling with his father taught him a "little more about real life" than most kids his age learned.

In the fall of 1939, Kuralt started kindergarten at St. Agnes Academy, a Catholic School across the Pamlico River. He showed early signs of being an independent thinker. A daring young man, he once asked the school's Sister Rosalind, "If thou shalt worship no graven images, then what are all those statues of the Virgin Mary and the saints doing around the school?" The other nuns frowned, but Sister Rosalind smiled. Though Kuralt was barely 5, she promoted him to the first grade. He later quipped that he heard his first French words at St. Agnes: "I remember the word for 'piano.' It is *piano*. I thought I could catch on to French if it continued that way."

An older cousin, Horace Gurganus remembers working with Charles at the Bishops' farm and finding his maturity amazing. When Charles was 6, he spoke like a 12-year-old, and when he was 12, he spoke like a high school graduate, Gurganus said. "He was so bright. He talked way over my head, and I was 14 years older. Where we boys around here talked about things right around us, Charles talked about worldly things, things he had read in the newspapers and in books."

L IVING IN WASHINGTON MEANT THE KURALTS were close enough to visit the Bishops' farm often. Summers, the Kuralts joined the hired hands to help out with the tobacco harvest. Charles was a "hander," putting together three or four leaves and passing them to a "stringer," who tied the ends with twine and twisted them around a stick. The tobacco sticks were then hoisted into a log barn for curing.

At the end of the tobacco season, the Bishops loaded their wagon with the golden brown leaves, hitched up the mule and took off with their grandson for the Kinston market, some 50 miles away. The trip offered Charles miles of adventurous thinking. On one trip, Rena Bishop told him about the old days of her childhood, when bandits robbed farmers returning home from the market. To thwart the bandits, wagons began to travel in groups, with a rifleman stationed on the lead wagon. Her story fired the youngster's imagination, and on the trips, he would pretend to be the armed guard, ever watchful for make-believe bandits.

"I remember the auction," Kuralt would write later in life, "the tension of it. A family's whole fortune for the year would be decided in a few seconds when the auctioneer stopped at the family's pile of tobacco."

Back at the farm, Charles plowed, or rather followed the mule down the furrow with a boy who taught him to sing, "There's a Star-Spangled Banner Waving Somewhere." He shucked corn. Finding a red ear entitled the shucker to kiss the girl of his choice. Of course, Charles was much too young to think about such things, but he enjoyed the camaraderie of shucking—the songs sung, stories told and riddles propounded.

With his father, Charles picked blueberries that grew in the ditches along the dirt road. Wallace imparted folk wisdom to his son: If you ask a Daddy Longlegs, "Where are my cows," he will raise a leg and point to them. You will be pretty

Charles, age 3, with many roads ahead.

if you wash your face in the dew of the first morning of May. When all men speak, no one hears. Many bring rakes, but few bring shovels. She's so thin she can't make a shadow. The first person to leave a funeral will be the next to die.

Down the road a poor black tenant farmer's son, Buck, taught Charles to ride his first bike, a Sears model he had received for Christmas. "He taught it by demonstration," Kuralt later said, "up and down the road, by the hour, calling back over his shoulder, 'See how easy it is?'"

Evenings, the Bishops and Kuralts gathered around a battery-powered radio, its round dial glowing orange with the station call letters—usually tuned to the nightly news broadcast on WPTF. News was all around. Stacked neatly on a nearby table were the weekly Onslow County newspaper and the *Raleigh News & Observer*.

As the family sat listening to voices telling tales from distant places, Charles dreamed of becoming a reporter, even playing out his dream by borrowing his father's hat and sticking a "press card" in its band. By age 6, Charles was convinced that reporting was a romantic profession that would take him to the exotic places his grandmother had read to him about.

> *A sandy road passed in front of the house and a logging path through the pinewoods behind it. I always wondered where the roads went, and after I learned that the one in front went to another farm a mile away, I wondered where it went from there.*
>
> —Charles Kuralt, *A Life on the Road.*

With his father's hat sitting squarely on his head, young Charles Kuralt seemed already to know those roads would one day become his home.

Charles Hoyt and the horse he refused to climb down from.

Flights of Fantasy

CHARLES HOYT
Childhood Friend

HEN WALLACE SR. WAS TRANSFERRED to Washington, North Carolina, the Kuralts settled into Green Court Apartments, just across the two-mile-wide Pamlico River, in the incorporated residential district of Washington Park.

The river and its banks provided fertile ground for young imaginations. On blistering hot days, neighborhood children splashed in the river to cool off, an activity requiring them to have typhoid shots three times a year. The kids took the "swimmin' shots" in stride—a necessary precaution, as upstream factories dumped their waste into the river.

Kuralt played with the neighborhood boys on the banks of the river, building tunnels, fishing, playing cowboys and looking for adventure. One day, the boys found part of a raft and launched themselves a little way down the river, but the adventure was short-lived. When they began drifting toward the current, the raft started to tip and the boys

Charles Kuralt became hooked on fishing at an early age, catching his first fish in the Pamlico River. Fishing would remain a lifelong passion.

had to jump for shore. Frightened, they swore never to tell their parents.

But it was not long before Kuralt and a friend were at it again, talking of building a raft to ride the river all the way out to Pamlico Sound and across to Ocracoke Island, a voyage of some 75 miles. Charles Hoyt remembers being conservative about the adventure, telling Kuralt: "That sounds dangerous. I know people who've drowned in the Pamlico Sound. You don't need to be doing that."

In the end, Kuralt gave up on that trip, but he continued to spend time on the river. On summer weekends, Kuralt and his father fished on the Pamlico River, trolling from a rowboat. One afternoon, Kuralt caught his first fish, a striped bass, fully five pounds. The bass flailed around in the bottom of the boat. "Hold on to him!" Wallace yelled. "I didn't know where to hold," Charles shouted in panic. "So I threw myself upon the fish," he later recalled, "weighted him down with my whole body and struggled all the way to the dock to prevent the fish from getting away."

With his catch in tow, Charles rushed home to show his mother. He slapped the fish in a wash pan and walked upstairs to a neighbor's apartment where his mother was meeting with the local garden club. "I caught him," Charles proclaimed proudly, thrusting the pan under his mother's nose. Knowing her son as mothers do, she accused him of buying the fish at a store and reached to touch it to prove her point. The bass flopped. His mother squealed. The boy beamed.

Later in life, Kuralt recalled his boyhood years in Washington with a vein of fantasy amid the facts. He liked to tell a story about playing cowboys with his friends, all riding broomsticks except for one older boy—it was Hoyt—who was rich and had a real horse for a horse. This friend also lived in a big white house by the river. "Since none of us had a horse,

At age 5, Kuralt played with the neighborhood boys on the banks of the Pamlico River, which runs parallel to Riverside Drive, shown here as it looks today. Though Green Court Apartments, where Kuralt lived, no longer exists, little else has changed. Stately Southern homes with large, wraparound porches face the river and the sunset over the water. Live oaks draped in Spanish moss stand amid crape myrtles and flowering dogwoods. In the shallows of the placid river, cypress trees pierce the water, their knotty knees punctuating the sandy shoreline. It was the perfect playground for the neighborhood boys.

and since he wouldn't climb down from his horse and ride a stick, we never played with him," Kuralt said. "I felt sorry for him, and wished to befriend him, but couldn't think of a way. It was my first experience with the camaraderie of the common people and the loneliness of the upper classes."

Hoyt still laughs about his old friend's "recollection." Hoyt's family did not live in a big white house by the river, but in a small house a few streets back. His horse, which Kuralt once referred to as a white horse like the Lone Ranger's, was "an absolutely atrociously ugly, viciously mean, shaggy Shetland pony named Bob," Hoyt said. The reason he refused to climb down from Bob, Hoyt added, was that the pony would kick him.

Charles Kuralt and family—sister Catherine, mother Ina, Charles, Wallace Sr. and Wallace Jr.

The Making Of
A Broadcaster

(The Charlotte Years, 1945–51)

T HE FAMILY DID NOT SETTLE DOWN for good until Kuralt was nearly 11. Until then, his father chased career opportunities that led the young family deeper into the South. Wallace signed on with the Social Security Administration as a public assistance analyst, a job that took him first to Birmingham, Alabama, in 1941, and then shortly thereafter to the federal agency's headquarters in Atlanta. In 1945 he quit, fed up with the agency's bureaucracy. The Kuralts were on the road again, heading back to their roots in North Carolina.

Leaving Atlanta temporarily interrupted Charles' journalistic career. He had been publishing his own neighborhood newspaper, *The Garden Gazette*, which he ran off on a mimeograph machine. The paper covered all the small-town news he could find—the birth of babies, the arrival of new people on the block. He hawked it to neighbors for two cents a copy.

Wallace Kuralt moved the family to Charlotte, where he became welfare superintendent of Mecklenburg County.

Kuralt credited his first journalism teacher, Anne Batten, left, with teaching him how to put together a first-rate newspaper. But it was Ransom Gurganus, a cousin of Kuralt's mother, who inspired him to pursue journalism. Gurganus, an amateur writer who had lived in New York and met Thomas Wolfe, encouraged Kuralt to begin his own newspaper, which he did as a 10-year-old in Atlanta—The Garden Gazette—and a year later in Charlotte—The Inquirer.

PHOTO OF ANNE BATTEN: TOM FRANKLIN STUDIO

The Inquirer

Published and Edited by Charles Kuralt
Edition 2 Volume 1
3¢ Per Copy
The Sharon Road Bi-Monthly

MORRISON STORAGE BARN DESTROYED BY FLAMES

On Saturday night, October 13, the Cameron Morrison storage barn, containing much valuable farm equipment, and over five tons of fertilizer was destroyed by fire.

Although the damage could be well in five figures, no official estimate has been made.

****

INQUIRER STAFF

"The Inquirer" announces its staff for 1945-46:

Editor - Charles Kuralt
Reporters - Bobby Butler
             Zeke Johnston
Staff Writer - Abbie Lockwood

****

SCHOOL SAFETY PATROL SWORN IN

Bulletin - The Sharon School Safety Patrol was officially sworn in on Thursday, October 11, in the school auditorium. Before the ceremony, moving pictures were shown by the County Police.

****

ED SPEAKS
By Charles Kuralt

In an effort to bring more and better news to its readers, "The Inquirer" announces a change in operation.

"The Inquirer" will henceforth be issued bi-monthly, and sell at a price of 3¢ per copy.

We hope that this will be a welcome change in "The Inquirer" publication.

****

RED CROSS FLAG RAISED

Bulletin - The Red Cross flag, bearing the emblem of the Red Cross, a red cross on a white background, was raised at Sharon School on Friday, October 12.

****

SMILE A WHILE

Friend: Where have you been recently?
Student: At college, taking medicine.
Friend: Did you finally get well?

****

Kuralt started seventh grade at Sharon School, near the seven-acre parcel of land the family purchased along Sharon Road, 10 miles south of the city. At last, they had made an investment in settling down.

His mother brought Kuralt by the hand for his first day in the new school, classmate Ruth Jones Pentes remembers. Ina Kuralt "wore her hair long and put up in a bun, which was very stylish at the time. Charlie wasn't very big. Of course, he was a year younger than everybody else," Pentes said, referring to his promotion back at St. Agnes.

The next year Pentes and Kuralt entered the eighth grade at Alexander Graham Junior High School. Anne Batten, Kuralt's English teacher and journalism counselor, recalled her former student's first year at the school. "He did what he always did in a new situation," she said. "He observed. If you look at the class picture at the end of the first year, he's looking around at everyone else. But by the ninth grade, he had observed and learned. The pictures at the end of that year show him to be much more confident and sophisticated."

I had several teachers before college who were encouraging to me. In eighth grade there was a teacher named Anne Batten, who was the journalism counselor to the little school paper that we put out. She made me believe that I could do good work, and there were others. Thinking back on that, I am pretty sure that's what people of that age—seventh-, eighth-, ninth-graders—need more than anything else. Just a little bit of encouragement. They need to believe, "This is something I can do." They need a compliment once in a while. Good teachers know how to bring out the best in students.

—Charles Kuralt, 1996 interview
Academy of Achievement

Batten remained forever impressed by her former pupil: "He had the writing skills and the ability to express himself," she said. "But I think his most important assets were his interest in people and his curiosity." Kuralt also developed a reputation for coming back from an assignment with a story, no matter what. When the celebrity he was supposed to interview at the bus station never arrived, Kuralt returned with a story about the bus station. "He could make a feature story out of anything," Batten said.

The next year, Kuralt rose to co-editor of the school paper, *The Broadcaster*, and wrote a front-page column he called "Kaleidoscope." To his classmates, this was very sophisticated stuff. Jack Claiborne said he had to look up the word "kaleidoscope" in the dictionary.

"Well, here I am again," Kuralt wrote in one of his first columns. "John Bulwark decided that editing this thing is too much of a mental strain, and all the good writers on the journalism staff had a lot of work to do and so, as you can see, ole Charley's back here trying to scrape up enough stuff to fill up this spot on the left-hand side of *The Broadcaster*."

Kuralt scraped up plenty. Among the topics were school dances, new students and report cards, sometimes his own. "It was real sport to sit back in my desk in Mrs. Ward's room wondering how many D's I'd get and watching the various expressions come on the faces of the luckless victims as they gazed at the bad news," he wrote in one column.

In another, he wrote about a school year of "highly contagious" fads: yo-yos and blue slip-over jackets, as well as blue slips of paper with the inscription, "I think we ought to come to school barefooted."

He wrote of spring, "And when you see a boy and girl leaving school together, with smiles on their faces just a little wider than the smiles of anybody else on the street, you know beyond a doubt that spring is here to stay." He wrote about getting into trouble. "You haven't lived until you have been tossed out of Miss Tomlinson's civics class for talking. We have lived."

Slowly, his style began to mature into that of a detached observer, a trademark of his reporting that he would master over the years. In one column, he described classroom scenes as if he were sitting in the corner observing: "Jack Chrisman reading a book entitled *Blood*. Freddie Collins shooting his cap pistol in journalism class. Dick Keeter daydreaming (about Joyce no doubt). Landon Smith humming 'Heartaches.'"

Near the end of his final school year at Alexander Graham Junior High School, Kuralt wrote a feature that provided a glimpse of things to come later in his career. Reminiscent of the type of people Kuralt would later profile "On the Road," he wrote about the school's maid, Rosa Calhoun, and her associate, Gertrude Dixon.

> *We found Rosa Calhoun sweeping the hall in front of the principal's office. Every afternoon she had been there as we passed, but we walked on without noticing her. This particular afternoon, though, we stopped ...*
>
> *... we'll be leaving A.G. soon, and in September a whole crop of new students will assemble in the auditorium, kind of doubtful and scared. And to greet them will be Rosa and 'Miss Gertrude'—two maids with a liking for their work, an interesting history, and two well-worn brooms.*

Kuralt was not yet dreaming of television, but his sights were aimed far beyond junior high. "Charlie used to talk about becoming editor of *The New York Times*," said Jean Alexander Chase, *The Broadcaster's* co-editor.

His booming voice opened many opportunities for him, said Alexander Graham Junior High teacher Anne Batten. He acted in the school's staging of a scene from "Romeo and Juliet" and was often asked to recite "Casey at the Bat." Pictured with Kuralt, classmate Jackie Jetton.

In 1947, he caught the attention of *Charlotte News'* sports editor Ray Howe, who let Kuralt write free-lance pieces. Kuralt was paid 10 cents for each inch of published copy. He received his first byline when he covered a junior high school basketball championship in Charlotte.

Kuralt was a *bona fide* reporter now, but he was still too young to drive himself to the games he covered.

> *My parents wouldn't even give me permission to own a motorbike. I rode the cross-town bus with my notebook showing out of my pocket and my typewriter prominent by my side, or yielded to the embarrassment to a ride to the gyms or football fields in the backseat of my parents' car, where the children always sat. I made this humiliation tolerable by imagining, there in the backseat, that I was flying across an ocean in a DC-3, checking over my notes for a big story while on the way to Constantinople or Khartoum.*
>
> —Charles Kuralt, *A Life on the Road*

Writing was not Kuralt's only passion in junior high. Batten remembers him as always "running to the next thing and never still." He was a popular student, winning election as vice president of his class. He was also class historian for the school yearbook, *Signing Off*. He acted in the school's Valentine's Day staging of a scene from "Romeo and Juliet." "He

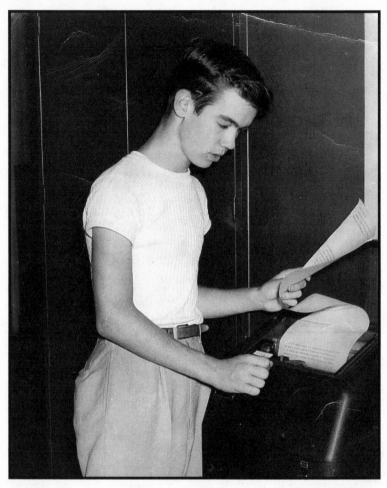

Scanning the news wire for sports material, 13-year-old Kuralt worked without pay at WAYS, where he had his own radio show, "Junior Sports Parade."

made quite an impression on the audience," Batten said.

He emceed school assemblies. He could recite "Casey at the Bat," complete with gestures and expressions, and was frequently asked to do so. "His booming voice and stage presence opened many opportunities for him," Batten said.

Mack Howey sometimes assisted Kuralt, who announced games for Charlotte's baseball team, the Hornets.

He was already working in radio and broadcasting sports events. In the spring of 1948, the *Charlotte News* reported that Kuralt, at age 13, was one of the youngest radio announcers in the country. In the press box at Griffith Park, Kuralt sat beside WAYS sportscaster Norman Young, giving between-inning color and summary for the Charlotte baseball team, the Hornets. Kuralt was often allowed to do the play-by-play. Once, when Young was out of town, the teenager called the play-by-play of the whole game.

Classmate Mack Howey assisted Kuralt that day. Kuralt thumped a cigar box with a pencil to simulate the sound of the bat hitting the ball. "I was aware that he was a bit unusual, a bit different, but to anticipate him becoming the 'Sunday Morning' host on CBS and one of the key people at the network—no, I didn't anticipate that," Howey said. "He did move to a different beat. He didn't just follow. He came up with his own thoughts and ideas and desires, and he'd follow those. It didn't make a great deal of difference to him what other people were doing or what they thought of what he was doing. He avoided fame and publicity. Those weren't the things that motivated him."

In 1948, ABC-affiliate WAYS gave 13-year-old Kuralt his own radio show, "Junior Sports Parade," every Tuesday after-

Charles "Abie" Lockwood remembers Kuralt as a fierce debater, not only on stage but also among friends.

noon during the summer. In 70-plus shows, all done without pay, he reviewed high school and junior high school sports, junior baseball league and city park activities.

Following his afternoon show, Kuralt and his pals Abie Lockwood, Landon Smith and Mack Howey would pile in a car to "drag main," cruising Morehead Street in a convoy of cars to the Town House. The drive-in was the hangout for Central High students, and over burgers and shakes, boys and girls would get to know each other. "Some of the girls we went to school with thought Charlie was completely stuck on himself," Lockwood said. "He really wasn't. They didn't know Charlie. He was too busy doing other things. He was more mature than we were. He was more involved in intellectual pursuits. He started working sooner than the rest of us. He wrote a lot. He was not boyish. He was more thoughtful and more involved in current events and politics and things of that nature than we were."

Kuralt began his sophomore year at Central High School, where he joined the Oratorical and Debating Society. He was fiercely competitive, arguing, for example, that if there was a hell, it was here on Earth. He irritated some of the fundamentalists, "but he would always make you come up with specifics," Lockwood said. "He wanted to know who we knew who was going to hell. You couldn't get away with generalizations."

Kuralt was ever eager for school to be out so he could go to work. "I loved working," he said in a 1996 interview. "And I suppose I was, in that way, a little bit of what would be called today a nerd. ... really I wasn't a very social boy. But I just loved writing and working at the radio station. I missed a good deal, I think. I certainly didn't pay as much attention in class as I should have."

Nonetheless, his writing and his ambition made him stand out. "We thought he'd become a newspaper reporter," Lockwood said. "Some thought he might become a radio correspondent. But all of us knew that he was destined for great things. You could just tell."

Kuralt wanted to be a sportswriter. He had hoped to write for the *Charlotte News* during the summer of 1948, but there was no opening. Writing a sports story, Kuralt said in a *Charlotte News* interview that year, gave him a bigger thrill than broadcasting. He confessed to some mike fright, telling the *News'* reporter: "I used to shake. Now I just talk, and I've learned to ad lib."

Jim Babb said his friend was no track star.

Despite those early tremors, his voice was beginning to take him places. In the fall of 1948, shortly after Kuralt began the 10th grade at Central High, the National Association of Broadcasters sponsored a contest that invited students across the country to write and deliver essays on the topic, "I Speak for Democracy." More than 250,000 students entered. As one of the four winners, Kuralt was invited to deliver his speech in the House of Burgesses in Colonial Williamsburg, Virginia.

But Kuralt did not excel at everything he tackled. Back at Central High School, he made the track team, but he was no star. Classmate Jim Babb described him as "dedicated, hardworking, but an average track man. It was probably the only thing he was average at in his whole life."

Ted Kemp, another Central High classmate, saw Charles in Spanish class, which, for Kuralt, was 45 minutes of pure terror. The teacher, Sarah Foster, "would walk up and down the aisles with a Spanish textbook in her hand, and you never knew when she was going to abruptly turn, point that pencil or finger at your nose and have you recite something in Spanish," Kemp said.

"Charlie didn't reveal a lot of himself to other kids" Kemp added, "but one day, he confessed to me, 'I haven't eaten lunch coming into this class for a long, long time, and I won't until the end of the year, because I just start throwing up. The thought of coming here makes me throw up, because I'm so scared of her.'"

It was odd to hear Kuralt speak of his schoolboy fears, because his voice was that of a grown-up, Kemp said. "It used to always amaze me," he added. "Here was this kid about my size and build, maybe 13 or 14 years old, and yet he had this incredible voice. He had the voice of an adult, even at that age, this deep, commanding voice that always seemed out of context, like it should not be coming from someone so young."

Kemp also saw Kuralt at Edith Kemp's Dancing School, where Kuralt and Sory Guthery took lessons under the tutelage of Ted's mother. "I can visualize them now doing the so-called 'forward together, side together,' learning the fox trot," Ted Kemp said. "Charlie was kind of a reticent, retiring young man, and Sory was a little that way, too. They showed a quiet interest in each other, but a very, very vast interest."

Sory and Charles had known each other since elementary school and seemed to be made for each other throughout their courtship in high school. In the 1951 Central High yearbook, the class prophecy accurately predicted, "Here is a good picture of the Kuralt family—Charlie married Sory Guthery."

It was a year of telling prophecies. At Central High, just as in junior high school, Kuralt was voted the student "Most Likely to Succeed." But although Kuralt had grand ambitions, he had no idea of just how far his success would take him. The journey along that road was just beginning.

100-YARD DASH MAN

Charlie hated me for introductions. I once introduced him for an event here in Charlotte before 2,000 or 3,000 people. I said, "You know, I got on my knees every day in high school before going to bed and thanked God for Charles Kuralt." And Charles, I could see, was getting emotional about what I was saying, and then I added, "Because he kept me from being the slowest 100-yard dash man in the state."

—Jim Babb, classmate, Central High

On the road trip with the Charlotte Hornets, Kuralt often played catch with Sonny Dixon, who would introduce the young reporter as "Flash Kuralt, our traveling big-time sportswriter." Like Kuralt, Sonny's talent also took him to New York, where he played for the Yankees.

Baseball Days

BUDDY CARRIER
Winner, "My Favorite Hornet"

WHEN KURALT WAS NOT WRITING for his junior high newspaper, he was entering writing contests, including "My Favorite Hornet," an annual affair sponsored by the *Charlotte News*. The newspaper invited boys 16 and under to submit 300-word stories about their favorite players on the city's minor league baseball team. The winner was rewarded with an invitation to travel for a week with the team.

In 1946, at age 12, Kuralt placed second to classmate and friend Jack Claiborne. The next year he finished second to Buddy Carrier. But that year Kuralt's eighth-grade essay on third baseman "Bouncing" Bobby Beal was impressive enough that he was invited to accompany Carrier on a six-day road trip with the Charlotte Hornets, a farm team for the major-league Washington Senators.

The two boys rode the team bus and took turns covering games in Asheville, North Carolina, and Knoxville,

Tennessee. "Every day we wrote a story about the trip, not a description of the game itself, but what it was like for ballplayers on the road, what they did and that kind of thing," Carrier said. "We were both excited about it, going on the trip and sitting in the dugout during the games with the players. It was a real thrill for a kid who was a big sports fan."

Kuralt called his column "Kuralt's Korner." From Knoxville, he filed his first story, headlined, "Umps Don't Know It When Cubans Heckle." He wrote, in part:

> *Knoxville, Tenn.—'Let 'er go, Newt.' Sonny Dixon shouted his favorite phrase as the Hornet bus pulled away from our hotel here in Knoxville Sunday afternoon and headed for Caswell Park.*
>
> *But when the bus returned after the 3 o'clock game with the Smokies, Sonny was not so jubilant. He had been batted out of the box in the second inning and was charged with an 8-3 loss in a game which saw Manager Cal Ermer thrown out and the Hornet bench cleared by Umpire Eddie Burke.*
>
> *It seems that riding an umpire is quite an art, and it is practiced only by certain members of the team, notably Kubuski, Dixon, Aloma, Del Monte and on occasion, Ermer himself. Aloma and Del Monte obviously have the edge in this custom, for the umpire doesn't know but what they are talking about the weather when, in reality, they are calling him names in Spanish ...*

When Carrier and Kuralt returned to Charlotte, they were invited to do a play-by-play broadcast of a Hornets game from Griffith Park. In a 1947 article titled, "Boys on Radio, But No One Hears Them," the *Charlotte News* reported:

Charles Kuralt, runner-up to Buddy Carrier in the Charlotte News' *Third Annual Sports Writing Contest, didn't know it when he was reciting a few verses about the frustrations of the mighty Casey on J.B. Clark's sports program last night, but he was fanning dead air also.*

The dinner-time thunderstorm had knocked WAYS off the air for a few minutes, and the entire program went to waste. … Kuralt, a runner-up for the last two years, blossomed out as a full-fledged entertainer when Clark, tipped off by several telephone calls, asked the 13-year-old to recite a few verses of "Casey at the Bat."

Charlie obliged and recited several verses complete with gestures before time caught up with him. The boys, however, were knocked out of their opportunity to do a play-by-play broadcast of a Hornet game, however, for last night's game was rained out …

Within a year, Kuralt had his own show at WAYS. As for Buddy Carrier, he makes a claim that few others can—that he once bested Charles Kuralt in a writing contest.

The pace of things seems too fast. More and more I think about Maine. I'd buy me a little bit of coast there, if I could, and sit there ... on the rocks. I did something like that on the day the men landed on the moon, but on Kauai .... tropical islands are too languid to concentrate upon. Maine is harder, better. I could write there, but I shall probably have to await my first heart attack.

—Charles Kuralt in a 1969 letter
to Barbara Simmons Hannah

Doubting Charles

BARBARA SIMMONS HANNAH
First Girlfriend

IN AN INTERVIEW A YEAR BEFORE HIS DEATH, Kuralt said he could not remember a time when he did not want to be a newspaper reporter. "From the first or second grade, I thought that's what I wanted to be, a reporter, a newspaper reporter, of course, because there was no television yet. And I never changed my mind."

His single-minded ambition took Kuralt far, but it also left heartache in its wake. Barbara Simmons Hannah was his teenage sweetheart, and when she talks about him some 50 years after their romance ended, her eyes betray the fact that she still is not completely over him.

She remembers the night the junior high newspaper colleagues fell in love. It was Friday, October 17, 1947. There was a dance at the Blue Room of the YWCA on East Trade Street in Charlotte. Barbara arrived with another writer from the school paper, Tommy Owens, who asked Charles to take a picture of him with his date. After firing off a shot of

Kuralt's first girlfriend, then Barbara Lee Simmons, had her own way with words as features editor of the junior high school paper that she and Kuralt worked on.

Barbara and Tommy, Kuralt extended his hand and invited Barbara to dance.

"The flash was still blazing in my eyes, and I looked up and jokingly asked, 'Who do you really like, Charlie?' And he said, 'You.' That's when I fell in love with Charlie Kuralt."

The courtship lasted nearly two years. The young couple spent long summer evenings, arm in arm, on Barbara's front porch swing. They talked, as innocent young romantics do, of their love for one another and even of getting married one day.

That day never came, and the relationship ended badly. Barbara believes it unraveled ultimately because Kuralt failed to win the "My Favorite Hornet" sportswriting contest, which, in a strange turn of events, she did.

After finishing second in 1946 and 1947, Kuralt decided not to enter in 1948. It was the worst outcome of all because the winner that year was his girlfriend. Barbara submitted a story about Hornets' third baseman "Bouncing Bobby Beal," the same player Kuralt had written about the year before. She signed her entry "Lee Simmons" in case the judges peremptorily threw out submissions from girls.

Kuralt did not share in the glory of Barbara's coup. That she had achieved where he failed was a great blow to his self-confidence. One evening, as they stood on her front porch saying good night, Kuralt hugged her longer and harder than usual. "I get so scared sometimes," he said with his face buried in her shoulder. "What if I don't make it?" The remark frightened her. "He was always so sure of himself," she said many years later. "I never realized he had feelings of insecurity like the rest of us."

Soon after that Kuralt broke off the relationship. Barbara tried to win him back, convinced that the split resulted from her winning the contest. (In a 1990 *Charlotte Observer* article,

Kuralt admitted to being "irritated" with Barbara for winning.) He told her it was too late; he already had someone else's picture on his dresser.

They met again in the early 1960s. Barbara was in New York visiting friends. Kuralt was eager to see her. Both were coming off failed marriages. Kuralt's had been to Sory Guthery, the "someone else" who took Barbara's place in his life a dozen years before.

The former sweethearts dined at a French restaurant. Kuralt regaled Barbara with stories about his work at CBS. It quickly became apparent that his job dominated his life. Leaning across the table, he confided a secret: "Someone from CBS once brought me here and said, 'I'm sorry, Charlie, but we're going to have to let you go. You don't write well enough.' It was the first time anything bad had ever happened to me."

Barbara could not believe what she was hearing. Kuralt was telling her that nearly losing his job was the first bad blow he had ever been dealt. "How could one get through childhood and adolescence without anything bad happening to them?" Barbara asked, reflecting on that conversation.

That evening, Barbara and Charles also talked of Charlotte and the old days, but invariably he returned to his ambitions. As they stood at a window in a penthouse bar overlooking Manhattan, watching the twinkling lights below, Kuralt said, "One day, everybody in this town is going to know who I am." Later he walked her to the subway. Waiting for the train, they embraced. "I remember standing there and kissing him," Barbara said. "We were falling in love all over again." But she returned to North Carolina the next morning and later married. The love that had been was left to linger.

The last time Barbara saw Kuralt was in 1987, 25 years after that evening in New York. This time, she came upon him

in Greenville, North Carolina, and they spent some time rem-
iniscing. As they parted, she said: "You know, I've always
loved you, but I'm glad we didn't get married. You would
have made a terrible husband."

Kuralt smiled and replied, "Yes, I suppose I've always been
a little self-destructive."

I consider myself successful, and certainly Charles was successful, but we just took separate paths. Charlie saw a world that many of us only dream about, but it was obvious that he missed some of the stableness of home. Still, I'll always remember his good, honest character, his thoughtfulness of others, and his deep desire to let the world be aware of the inner beauty of individuals and all God's creations. He knew how to view the color of the world. He truly lived his life "On the Sunny Side of the Street."

—Landon Smith

Two Roads Diverged

LANDON SMITH
Best High School Friend

K URALT MET LANDON SMITH in the sixth grade, and the two would remain best friends through high school. Afternoons and weekends, they shot a basketball through the hoop mounted on the Kuralts' garage. They listened to jazz records on a Victrola. They went to the bowling alley and to Central High football games. They sat down for banana splits in Walker's Drug Store and pulled their cars up to the curb for burgers and shakes at the Town House.

It was a glorious, carefree time, but it was also a time when both boys were beginning to take separate paths. As a 14-year-old sophomore, Kuralt was a busy and popular student who was also working as a disc jockey for WAYS.

"We were told he was the youngest radio announcer in the United States," Smith said, adding that Kuralt used the hit song "On the Sunny Side of the Street" to kick off his evening program. The song became his identity. The young DJ "talked slightly faster than he did in later years," Smith said, "but he

Charles Kuralt (third from left, front row) and Landon Smith (third from right, third row) were best friends from the sixth grade at Sharon School, where this picture was taken, through Central High School. In high school, Smith tolerated Kuralt's squeaking on the clarinet.

was always clear, concise, pleasing and relaxing. He made you think. He would give you personal tidbits and historical facts about the musicians whose music he played."

Kuralt found not only musicians fascinating but also ordinary people. On nights when Smith slept over, the boys cut photographs of people from the *Charlotte News* and spent hours concocting stories about them. "Charles liked to talk about people and put himself in their place," Smith said. "He'd ask, 'Well, what's this person like? What do you think his business is? What type of character does he have?'"

At other times, Smith suffered the incessant squeaking of Kuralt's clarinet practice, and he allowed Kuralt to correct his diction. In some ways, the two posed striking contrasts. Smith delivered the *Charlotte News*. Kuralt wrote for the paper. Smith piddled with his motorbike. Kuralt tapped away on the typewriter that he carried to school each day. Smith joined the Navy. Kuralt went to college.

But Kuralt was drawn to his friend's sense of adventure, and accompanied him on "Landon's Revue of Wonders," a traveling amateur magic show performed for church groups, birthday parties and talent shows. Kuralt was Smith's assistant and the revue's emcee.

While Smith practiced his magic, Kuralt practiced his voice, imitating Edward R. Murrow and other leading broadcasters. "He could imitate the best of them," Smith said.

Both were natural performers, and they occasionally organized daredevil shows, charging neighborhood kids a dime admission. They were fearless. One stunt called for Smith to jump his motorbike from one ramp to another, a distance of 10 feet. To heighten the thrill, Kuralt and two other kids stretched out on their backs between the two ramps. Smith revved up the bike and flew across the chasm without scraping a single belly.

Landon Smith and Charles Kuralt both enjoyed performing. Working afternoons at WAYS, an ABC affiliate, Kuralt kicked off his broadcast with the hit song, "The Sunny Side of the Street." Smith worked magic in "Landon's Revue of Wonders," for which Kuralt served as the emcee.

Smith had acquired the motorbike to work his paper route, but he and Kuralt clocked a lot of miles on the little machine, joy riding around the Mecklenburg County countryside. When they couldn't afford gasoline, Smith made off with dry-cleaning fluid from his mother's closet to fuel the bike.

But a couple of accidents brought the motorbiking buddies back to earth. First, Smith collided with the Kuralts' house. He escaped unscathed, but a couple of days later, the front wheel fork broke on the bike. The newspapers he was delivering went everywhere, and he flew 50 feet over the front of the machine, ending up in the hospital with a skinned knee. "After that, Charlie and I did a lot of thumbing for rides," Smith said.

Kuralt desperately wanted wheels. A few months before his 16th birthday, he started nagging his father to help him get a driver's license early. Wallace eventually sighed defeat and signed a notarized statement swearing that his son's birthday was June 1, almost four months ahead of Kuralt's 16th birthday.

The license gave the high school friends the freedom they craved, and they set out on an extended car trip to California and the Golden West. But halfway across the country, the journey began to go awry. The young adventurers were suffering "crises of inexperience," Kuralt wrote in *A Life on the Road*. They had overestimated the car's soundness, the distance they could travel in a day and their own immunity to homesickness. After crossing the Mississippi, he and Smith pointed their 1938 Chevy north and headed toward Evanston, Illinois.

There, at Northwestern University, Kuralt attended a six-week writing program for high school students while Smith, at least according to Kuralt, sold hot dogs to make enough money to go home. With Smith gone, Kuralt said, he finished his studies, then caught the train to Gary, Indiana, where he lugged his "big Samsonite suitcase to the side of the highway and started hitchhiking home."

Smith said his friend's account of the trip "made a good book," but differed markedly from his own recollection. According to Smith's memory, the boys left Evanston together in their Chevy and made a circuit of Niagara Falls, New York, Washington, D.C., and Montreal before returning to Charlotte. "We went to a Broadway show in New York and the Smithsonian Institute in Washington," Smith said. In Montreal, "we had trouble getting directions" because everyone spoke French.

If, during that summer of 1950, Kuralt was struggling with Canadian French instead of hitching rides home from the Midwest, it throws serious doubt on the stories he wrote later about the elderly couple and the "kindly and demented evangelist" he met along the way home. It would mean he did not pattern his life "after that of the daft old man in the pickup, who wandered where the back roads took him."

Whose story is true? Charlotte classmate Ruth Jones Pentes remembers the boys arriving home together.

Maybe the facts eluded Kuralt's memory. Or maybe, to smooth the transition to the next chapter in his book, he substituted a series of events from one time in his life for those of another. Maybe he really did hitch a ride with the daft old man, but years further down the road. Or maybe he was only telling a good story. We will never know.

What is known is that Kuralt and Smith started down the same road together, but their paths diverged, and, as in the Robert Frost poem, Kuralt took "the one less traveled by." They eventually lost sight of each another.

Smith became an electronic engineer with AT&T, has been married to the same woman for more than 40 years and raised two children. Kuralt joined CBS and became extraordinarily successful, at the expense of his first family.

Thirty-seven years after their road trip together, Smith caught up with Kuralt at a Holiday Inn in Greensboro, North Carolina. The conversation was "kind of cool," Smith recalled. "Charles was a little more reserved." Another time, Smith and his wife were visiting New York and called Kuralt at his Brooklyn apartment. He told them to come on over. "We did," Smith said, "but in just five minutes, he was out the door to catch a plane."

The sense of loss was, and still is, great for Smith. Maybe too much was left unsaid. He remembers giving Kuralt a black eye many years back, and wonders if that created the rift between them. "He probably never forgave me for that, and I can't blame him," Smith said. "Now, 50 years later, I can't remember why it happened. I hope he can see this. I'm sorry, Charlie."

As teenagers, they talked about driving to New Orleans. Kuralt loved Dixieland jazz and idolized Louis Armstrong, Dizzy Gillespie, Pete Fountain and other jazz greats. Years later, Smith moved to New Orleans, and for the next decade, he kept hoping that Kuralt would visit. "We could have had a ball together."

He kept hoping, too, that the old friendship could be rekindled. In later years, Smith and three other Central High classmates hosted reunions in the North Carolina mountains. Kuralt was always invited but never came. At the spot reserved for their old friend, they placed Kuralt's picture.

As a high school student, Kuralt worked at ABC-affiliate WAYS; later, while at UNC-Chapel Hill, he came back to Charlotte during the summers to work at WBT, a CBS affiliate.

News Writer

BROOKS LINDSAY
Radio Disc Jockey, WAYS

B ROOKS LINDSAY SHOWED UP FOR HIS regular shift at WAYS on a June afternoon in 1951 and found Kuralt pecking away on an old Royal typewriter. Curious as to what was going on, he asked, "Charlie, what's up?" Kuralt replied, "Oh, Harry asked me to do a bio on Julian Barber."

A few days earlier, radio announcer Julian Barber had done an outstanding story about a possible cease-fire in the Korean war. Now ABC wanted to do a profile of Barber, who had once worked at ABC-affiliate WAYS. So ABC contacted the station's program manager, Harry Barfield, who assigned the job of writing the bio to 16-year-old Kuralt.

"Charlie looked like Schroeder, the kid in the Peanuts series who plays the piano," Lindsay said. "He was just banging away." Lindsay saw that Kuralt had crossed out words and added others. There were markings all over the page—a real mess. He watched as Kuralt ripped the draft from the typewriter and typed a final revision. Lindsay was sure the young writer was going to have to do a major revision. Kuralt handed the copy to Barfield, who sent it over the news wire to ABC headquarters. At 6 o'clock, ABC began its news broadcast from New York, and the crew listened as John Daly read the Barber bio. When the broadcast was over, Lindsay turned to Barfield and asked how much was cut. "Harry said to me very quietly, 'Not a word,'" Lindsay said. "I knew then who Charles Kuralt was."

Lindsay saw further evidence of Kuralt's talents on Friday nights. Working the late-night shift, "doing a soupy radio program with soft music and quiet words," Lindsay said Kuralt would occasionally drop by the station to take part in the program. The young man liked to walk out onto a fire escape off the studio, look out over the city and just talk. "We'd hang a mike on him," Lindsay said. "And he would literally create poetry without notes or anything. He just looked out at the city and described it."

Lindsay often invited the teenager to his house for breakfast on mornings following their broadcast together. Kuralt used the opportunity to pick the veteran broadcaster's brain. "He was an intellectual sponge," Lindsay said. "He would ask you questions in a nice way, you know, just in a conversation, and then he would sit there and listen to you. He would not try to add to your conversation. He would listen as the Navajos do, until you get through, you know. Then he'd ask the proper questions. That was his genius."

L INDSAY LAST SAW KURALT IN 1994. Kuralt had just wrapped up 37 years at CBS and was standing at the Hertz counter at the Charlotte airport. He had come home to write a chapter of his book, *Charles Kuralt's America*. Lindsay, who worked part-time at the airport's welcome center, picked up a microphone and announced over the public-address system, "Will the recipient of the Ernie Pyle Award please come to the welcome center." (In 1957, as a reporter at the *Charlotte News*, Kuralt won the Ernie Pyle Memorial Award, which recognized excellence in journalism.)

Kuralt walked over, looking very tired. He failed to recognize the man he once worked with, even after Lindsay tried to remind him of their days at WAYS. Kuralt finally let out a sigh. "He looked ill and acted that way," Lindsay said. "And so I said, 'I didn't want to take up your time.' I just sort of sloughed it off and said hello to him and let it go at that."

THE WRETCHED BOOK TOUR

Among Kuralt's earliest radio influences was Norman Corwin, once described by Ray Bradbury as "the greatest director, the greatest writer and the greatest producer in radio history." In August of 1995, Kuralt wrote to Corwin about finishing his new book, *Charles Kuralt's America:*

> *I came back here and typed until the gray dawn with your language in my head, which helped, and two martinis in my belly, which didn't seem to hurt much, and I sent the last of my book off to the publisher the next day. It may not be very good, but it's finished. I'm going to try never to accept a deadline again. The worst of it is that in October and November I have to go about praising myself on talk shows in order to sell the book.*
>
> *Writing it ought to be enough. The book tour is a wretched undignified ritual, though I suspect I'll run into Colin Powell and Pat Conroy similarly whoring around the country ...*

At WAYS, Kuralt narrated "The Report," a weekly recap of the news. Although he was only a kid, he had the confidence of an adult and a mature voice to match.

The Impressive, Impressionable Kid

KEN MCCLURE
Radio Writer, WAYS

D URING HIS SENIOR YEAR OF HIGH SCHOOL, Kuralt worked
for WAYS radio on a Sunday evening program called
"The Report," a review of the news of the week. The
program opened with a clock ticking and Kuralt reading a few
lines from the *Rubáiyát of Omar Khayyám*.

> *The Moving Finger writes; and, having writ,*
> *Moves on: nor all thy Piety nor Wit*
> *Shall lure it back to cancel half a Line,*
> *Nor all thy Tears wash out a Word of it.*

A review of the show that Kuralt narrated appeared in
Variety magazine, which identified the young radio personality as possessing a "resonant voice" with a "surprisingly
mature quality."

The copy for "The Report" was written by Ken McClure,
a member of the 5,000-watt station's news and promotions

𝕿𝖍𝖊 𝕯𝖆𝖎𝖑𝖞 𝕿𝖆𝖗 𝕳𝖊𝖊𝖑
UNIVERSITY OF NORTH CAROLINA
CHAPEL HILL
FROM THE DESK OF
THE EDITOR

ANY MENTION FROM YOU MIGHT HELP. UNITED PRESS
JOB FELL THRU WHEN UNIPRESS CUTS BUEDGET.
PARA THIS JOB LOT OF FUN BUT GRUELLING DEAL
SPENDING TEN-TWELVE HOURS A DAY ON PAPER TRYING
GO CLASSES STUDY TOO. WE HAD FRAT HOUSE
SHOOTING SUICIDE OTHER DAY EYE CVRED ASSOCIATED
PRESS NY DAILY NEWS (THE NEWSPAPER THAT READS
FASTR AND LIVELIER) SENT STAFFERS DOWN EYE
WATCHD BIG TIMERS OPRATE BIG KICK FOR HICK KID.
EYE NOW DOING AP THINK PEECE ON EFFECTS END
SEGRGATION ON UNIVERSTY COMMUNITY YOU WATCH
IN SCRIPPS HOWARD RAG EL PASO. NY TIMES, CHARL
NEWS REPRINTED SEGRGATION EDIT SWELLING HED
EVN BIGGR THAN USUAL. PARA. ON OTHR FRONTS:
MARRIAGE COMING OFF AUG 25 MYRS PARK BAPTST
CHRCH CHARL WE FOUND RENOVATED TNANT SHACK
ON EDGE OF TOWN IT EVEN HAS INSIDE PLMBING
JUST SHOW YOU HOW WE GOING FRST CLASS ALL WAY.
WE INSTALLING FRNTURE, STOVE, RERGRATOR,
INTERWORLD MACHINE THIS SUMMR. EYE TLKED SORY
LAST NITE SHE SAY THNKS FOR YOUR HELLO'S AND.

In a letter typical of those Kuralt sent to his buddy Ken McClure, the young editor of The Daily Tar Heel *talks of his syndicated story on segregation that was picked up by the large newspapers, his upcoming wedding and his move to a cabin on the edge of town.*

staff, but Kuralt edited the pieces, crossing out sections and adding others. "I was impressed with that, because you don't expect such confidence from a teenager," McClure said. "That's when I began to think that this guy's got tremendous potential."

Even though Kuralt was younger than McClure by more than a decade, they struck up a friendship that lasted through Kuralt's college years. The two exchanged letters written in a shorthand language they called "cable-ese." They picked up the idea from a book, *Kansas City Milkman*, about a couple of reporters who filed their stories by cable telegram. Kuralt sent a "cable-ese" letter to McClure in May 1954 to announce his rise to editorship of the UNC student newspaper, *The Daily Tar Heel*: "Swelling hed evn biggr than usual."

In another cable-ese letter to McClure, who by then had moved on to a radio station in El Paso, Texas, Kuralt wrote that a CBS News job looked like a sure bet after graduation.

"They nice people," Kuralt wrote in the arcane language. "Remember my name three trips Washington urge me keep in touch stop face it colon eye still impressionable kid stop." In an October 15 letter to McClure, Kuralt wrote about the "glorious upchange in leaves red yellow brown ..." and he added how happy he was that girlfriend Sory Guthery was coming to Chapel Hill for the weekend to walk in the leaves. "Fall in love all over again."

Kuralt, second from right, was one of four national winners in the "I Speak for Democracy" contest, sponsored by the National Association of Broadcasters. The contest prize included a visit with President Harry Truman. In later years, Kuralt wrote to friend Wesley Wallace that he thought he had written something "lasting and immortal" at the time.

Voice Of Democracy

―――

JACK CLAIBORNE
High School Friend

IN 1948 JACK CLAIBORNE WATCHED KURALT give his winning speech "I Speak for Democracy" for classmates at Central High School. "That was such a thunderclap of notoriety for someone in high school to have won," Claiborne said, "especially someone as young as Charles was."

Kuralt looked younger than his age and was in fact younger than his classmates, thanks to his early start in first grade. But the language, the tone, the substance of the speech was anything but boyish. It was "not the kind of language people my age would have used," Claiborne said. "That immediately put Charles in another category."

The contest prize included a trip, which Kuralt made with his mother, to the White House to meet President Harry Truman. In a 1996 interview, Kuralt recalled that trip: "I still have a photograph of a very congenial President Harry Truman ... and me, both of us wearing neat blue, double-breasted suits, the fashion of 1948," he said. "That contest, and doing well in it to my surprise, added to my confidence. It made me think, 'I can do this. I can write and speak with anybody my age.' It was a great confidence builder. It did have an important effect in my life."

Charles and his mother retired to Washington's Statler Hotel after what they thought was the end of an unbelievable day. But more was ahead. They were told to make sure they did not miss Edward R. Murrow's broadcast that evening. The CBS Radio legend always ended his broadcast with "A Word for the Day," and that night he quoted Kuralt's winning essay.

"That was a great thrill, because Murrow was a hero in our family," Kuralt said. "I think my mother was especially proud that Murrow quoted her son on the air. Years later, when I became briefly a very junior colleague of Ed Murrow's, I told him that story, and it just delighted him. He went about telling it to everybody. To think that he had quoted me on the air, and here I was working for CBS News a few years later."

KURALT AND CLAIBORNE'S PATHS would cross again after college. Claiborne became an editor at the morning paper, the *Charlotte Observer*, while Kuralt was writing for the afternoon *Charlotte News*. Each year, the *News* published a special progress edition, designed primarily to attract advertisers. But Kuralt took everything he wrote seriously, and when he wrote the lead story for the 1956 special edition, it won a statewide contest. "Charles valued words and what he put on paper so much that even writing something like a throwaway piece, he put a first-class effort into it," Claiborne said.

Think about Charlotte, the big proud city, the hub with two long spokes over two states. But use your imagination. Do not think about Charlotte as it is, but picture it without, say, the concrete ribbon of Independence Blvd.

Think about it without the green acres of Freedom Park,
without the mammoth, modernistic Auditorium-Coliseum or
the airport terminal or the Jefferson Standard Building.

Conceive of the city minus 17 schools, 500 stores and
50,000 people. Take away … a couple of dozen churches
and most of the suburban shopping centers. Take away most
of the suburbs.

Reduce the city limits several blocks on all sides. Take
the television sets from every house where there is one.

Now you are beginning to get there …

… what you have when you are finished is Charlotte,
still, but Charlotte on Jan. 31, 1946—10 years ago today.
…

At the *Charlotte News*, Kuralt began to apply his talents to
an award-winning column called "People." He wrote about
ordinary people who might otherwise have gone unnoticed,
just like the two maids he had written about as a ninth-grader
back at Alexander Graham Junior High School.

"He was looking for those themes, those ideas that
expressed something larger than what you normally find in
the run-of-the-mill newspaper and the run-of-the-mill TV
news show," Claiborne said. "Charles had such insight,
insight into people, insight into situations. It was as if he had
a magnifying glass that made things larger and showed him
things that the rest of us didn't see or didn't feel. He was very
perceptive."

Those abilities eventually landed Kuralt at CBS, which,
surprisingly, disappointed Claiborne and a few others in
Charlotte. Claiborne, for one, thought CBS was unworthy of
Kuralt. "Writers were not the kind of thing that you had at
CBS. I thought back to his voice. It was his father's voice. And

I felt like he was trading on a talent that was lesser than the writing skills that he had. And yet we all watched to see what was going to happen, and we were very pleased to see that Charles started doing a program called 'Eyewitness to History.'"

Just a few months into that program, though, Kuralt lost the anchor job to Walter Cronkite and was shipped off to Rio de Janeiro, as the only CBS correspondent on the whole continent of South America. "I was sorry that this was happening to him, because I thought Charles was better than that," Claiborne recalled. "I would see Charles, instead of writing for CBS, writing for *The New Yorker* or the *Saturday Evening Post.*"

But in 1979, with the debut of CBS's "Sunday Morning," Kuralt found a medium to express his unique perspectives and display his talented writing. "'Sunday Morning' reeked of the best in Charles, his understanding of politics, his understanding of culture and the arts, his understanding of people and his ability to draw them out," Claiborne said. "The exchanges he would have with the guests, or some commentary about movies or some commentary about the news, those little exchanges were very revealing of the depth and the seriousness with which Charles was going about his work. It was often that his remarks said something more. They told you that Charles was fully aware of what was happening. He was sort of the puppeteer controlling the broadcast."

During Kuralt's final days at CBS, he and Claiborne talked a couple of times. Claiborne could sense that his old friend was growing tired of the network's demands. One conversation took place before Kuralt left to cover the Winter Olympics. Claiborne asked Kuralt: "Just what in the world are you doing going to the Olympics? What are you going to do?

"I knew he no longer wrote anything about sports or was interested, and he said, 'Well, they've got the crazy idea that

I will be able to put some of this in perspective.' But, he said, 'I am asking the same question you are, "Why am I going?" I always thought that that was a misuse of him."

Another conversation followed Kuralt's decision to leave CBS for good. He told Claiborne he was hoping to do more writing. Claiborne hoped so, too: "I hoped without the deadlines, without the demands of television and 'Sunday Morning' that he would be free to write more things that fulfilled those expectations those of us saw in him, this enormous talent, when he was writing those 'People' columns."

Of course, that was not to be—Kuralt died three years after leaving CBS.

I SPEAK FOR DEMOCRACY
BY CHARLES KURALT, 1948

We, the people of the United States, the Constitution talking, the United States Constitution, bulwark of the greatest democracy on earth. We, the people, ruling ourselves, running the government. We the people, 48 States, one Nation. We the people, thousand upon thousand of common men. We made this Nation—a land where anyone, anything, any idea can grow, unchained and free. Great things have been said and written about this thing called democracy, but democracy is more than a written word or a spoken phrase. It is men created equal. Democracy is very evident. It is written in the faces of immigrants, the people who gave up hopes in the old country to try out something new and wonderful. It is written in the very hills and plains that have produced men like Abraham Lincoln. It is written in our lives—our brothers and ourselves growing up with a chance.

We hold these truths to be self-evident, that all men are

created equal. That they are endowed by their creator with certain inalienable rights, that among these are life, liberty and the pursuit of happiness and freedom of thought and speech from want and fear. Inalienable rights guaranteed in this democracy.

Inalienable right number one is life—something men have cherished from the beginnings of the earth, a free life, unfettered by government interference. It's what Americans fought for at Lexington and Bunker Hill and New Guinea and the Solomons. But they were fighting for something more, something that we will call inalienable right number two—liberty. That's a big word in the American language. It's the first cousin of another big word—freedom.

Liberty is guaranteed in America. It flourishes here as in no other country in the world. The unknown little man mounting his soap box to speak his piece about how the country ought to be run. The editor of a small-town daily writing as he pleases, condemning or commending the administration freely. This little group of Mormons or Quakers or Jews worshipping God in their own way. The scientist free to search for truth, and the educator, free to teach it.

Liberty and freedom and democracy—big words in the language of a people. We take them for granted; they are ours. They build the third inalienable right championed by Thomas Jefferson—the pursuit of happiness. People living everywhere looking for a good life. People in little towns with funny names, people in the metropolis living beside the water or the highway, looking for a good life.

One people—all races, all stocks, simple people, but easy to rile up if you talk about taking away their freedom. We know what freedom is in America, and democracy—don't tread on us. It's produced great men—this democratic government, this youngest of the earth's powers—great names like George Washington and Thomas Jefferson and F. D. R. and Babe Ruth. And in song and in prose, the men it has produced have expressed their views of the nation's politics. James Russell Lowell called a democracy a place where every citizen has a chance and knows he has it.

Woodrow Wilson said he believed in democracy because it releases every one of man's powers, and James Pike, putting it into the words of the Louisiana Negroes, said the same thing, in a different way.

"Freedom" he said, "is a patient word, a prayerful word, a good tasting word, a sparkling word, as full of the Fourth of July as skyrockets and roman candles. Freedom is a word, a real showboat word, eight dollars long and four dollars wide."

And so that is my case—I give you democracy—not a word, not essentially a type of government. It is warm rain on Georgia, sun shining on Key West. It's wind blowing over a Texas prairie, snow-capped Massachusetts hills, the sound coming up from the streets of Manhattan, waves roaring in on California's coast, industry in Chicago, and hot steel in Pittsburgh. The names of Michigan and Maryland, of Virginia and Rhode Island and North Carolina. Covered wagons rolled West, with democracy for a dream.

Democracy is a way of life, a living thing, a human thing comprised of muscles and heart and soul. I speak for democracy, and men who are free and men who yearn to be free speak with me.

You know, most reporters can't go back to the towns they've written about. I never wrote that kind of story.

—Charles Kuralt
1994 interview

Downtown: Saturday Night, December 24, 1949

BY CHARLES KURALT

THE FOLLOWING ESSAY, published in the April 1950 issue of *North Carolina English Teacher*, was written by Kuralt in the 11th grade, age 15.

'Tis the night before Christmas. 'Tis evening of a gloomy Saturday that is cold and wet. In the parks the trees stand firm, their bare boughs creaking in the wind. The sky is overcast; the damp wind sniffs at every lamp post and deserted alleyway.

In the big churchyard on Trade Street, the rocks are wet. The gravel paths, clean from many rains, are neat against the dead brown of faded grass. Mist falls upon the asphalt.

In the windows of all the stores, the "Merry Christmas" signs hang, their silvered lettering staring out on the street. The neon gets mixed up in the mist. In one shop window, dressers in felt slippers are already at work, taking away the displays, getting ready for the big post-Christmas sales. They take down the fake holly wreaths, cotton, silver dust, and speak choppily to each other, their mouths full of pins.

The buses (10 MIDWOOD, 9 EASTOVER, 2 OAKHURST, 7 SECOND WARD) pull to a stop beside the jewelry store on the square. It is a cold night; nobody wants to be downtown. The buses are empty when they arrive, full of people as they pull away.

Oh, the side streets are the coldest! Jake Bowers knows it. Jake walks along Church Street, stands on the corner of Fourth, takes his hands from his pockets and begins blowing on his fists. Jake is broke. His overalls are frayed, his hair is long, and he is getting thin. He shuffles in the cold, watches an auto skim along the wet pavement, and thinks about wheatcakes. When he reaches the mission, his mind is warm with wheatcakes, but his legs are like wood.

The Yuletide is going on. The lights in front of the mission are put out, all except one single bulb that burns brightly over the doorway near a gilt sign which reads, "Jesus Saves." Inside, in a corner, the tin cups used for stew are piled up on the floor; and a few feet away, the folding chairs are lined up. The twenty-dollar upright piano used for hymn singing is locked tight. The manager has the key; it swings from a shiny silver ring and hangs inside his vest. On the sidewalk in front of the mission, half obliterated by the dampness of the weather, is a passage from the Scriptures printed in many colors of chalk—red, green, purple, white, and old rose: "What does the Lord require of thee but to love mercy, do justice, and walk humbly ... "

Toward midnight, the air grows damper, the chalk marks blur, running together, and all that is visible is "walk humbly." No more, or less. The heavy sign above the movie distributor's down the street begins to sway slightly when the wind shifts.

Two old bums stand in a grocery store doorway. "Where you goin'?" the first one says.

"Me?"

"Yeah, you."

"I'm goin' to sleep," the second one answers and walks up into the doorway. "Where you goin'?" he says, stretching out on the damp tiles, moving his bones around to find a nice, soft tile or two.

"I'm gonna sleep, too," the first one says and ambles up, shuffling his old varicose legs, settling down before his pal.

Across the way, the bulb burns brightly: "Jesus Saves." The light is in their eyes. They turn their backs toward it.

Over on Trade Street, the church with the big yard begins ringing its bells. Christmas morning steals along like a gray wolf sneaking into a dead prairie town at dawn. Panes of glass rattle in their sockets. A roomer from the second floor goes tramping down the stairs, turns the knob, and slams the door, while outside the street lamps throw their cold white glare.

Charles would get off work from the radio station late at night and ride the bus to the end of the line, and rain, snow or heat, he would walk the rest of the way home. Nobody babied him or took responsibility for him. He did it himself. I think that made a man of him. So many boys his age were not capable.

—Mrs. George Heaton

Baptism Into Storytelling

C.D. SPANGLER

President Emeritus, UNC

YERS PARK BAPTIST CHURCH was not what you would call a typical Southern Baptist church. While battles over dogma were consuming other congregations in the Bible Belt, Myers Park kept its distance. Instead, the church's young minister, George Dewitt Heaton, was attracting national attention for his liberal views on religion and race—and his encouragement of inquisitive thought.

Heaton made a believer out of Kuralt, who admitted that he attended Sunday school purely to hear George Heaton talk. "It's as simple as that," Kuralt told the *Charlotte Observer* in 1983. "I now realize, looking back, that he was talking about things that had been debated by the great Christian philosophers through the ages."

Kuralt was amazed that Heaton would take the time to talk about such things with teenagers. And Heaton was effective in communicating these ideas to the young people. "He took the time to get to know us," Kuralt said. "He could find

Dr. George Heaton of Myers Park Baptist Church, and his wife often invited Charles Kuralt and other teenagers to their home. Mrs. George Heaton remembered being particularly impressed by Kuralt's work ethic.

the right way to put things to get ideas to stick to us. We had a sense of momentum. We were like a bunch of dogs that hung around by the church steps. We were too excited to go home."

Another young man who came to hear Heaton speak was C.D. Spangler, who went on to become president of UNC. Spangler witnessed firsthand the great influence the minister had on Kuralt. "He revered his relationship with Dr. Heaton, and in some ways, he probably followed Dr. Heaton's format in storytelling," Spangler said. "Dr. Heaton was a good listener, but he combined that with this marvelous ability to tell stories. Having sat in that Sunday school class and watched the two of them, I am quite confident that Charles picked up a lot of that from Dr. Heaton."

Heaton captivated the teenagers with stories about unusual people, the same kind of people Kuralt himself would later be drawn to write about. The minister told about his visit to a factory that employed blind workers and his interview there with a woman who tied knots in nylon thread all day long. Heaton asked how she coped with the monotony of the work, and she replied, "Every knot I tie has to be perfect, because these go in tires for airplanes, and the pilot would be killed if these threads broke."

Kuralt, like Heaton, had a mesmerizing voice, but Spangler believes Kuralt's thoughts and storytelling abilities "clearly were the essence of his power."

"His voice was only an instrument to put those thoughts forth—sort of like Beethoven wrote his symphonies on paper, but somebody had to play it through violin and horns," Spangler said. "Charles' voice was only an instrument to get his thoughts into consideration."

Ruth Jones Pentes' friendship with Kuralt spanned from the seventh grade until his death. Once sweethearts, they remained close pals. In later years, Kuralt began to envy her settled life. He was clearly beginning to think about what he had missed in his life on the road.

School Days

———

RUTH JONES PENTES
Lifelong Friend

A FTER HIGH SCHOOL, CHARLES KURALT went north to Chapel Hill. Ruth Jones Pentes, his friend from his first day at Sharon School, went farther north—to Oberlin College in Ohio. But when the old friends met over Christmas break, Kuralt's nonstop chatter about UNC made Ruth want desperately to go to school there, too.

But UNC excluded female students until their junior year. So Ruth signed up for the fall semester at The Woman's College of the University of North Carolina in Greensboro with the intention of transferring to UNC after her sophomore year. As it happened, Sory Guthery, Ruth's friend from childhood and Kuralt's soon-to-be bride, was a student there, too. Because of that, Ruth saw a lot of both of them.

Kuralt often borrowed a fraternity brother's car to visit his fiancée in Greensboro. "There was a golf course that belonged to the college out beyond the dorms," Pentes recalled. "I can see them now, gamboling across that green golf course on weekends. They were just madly in love."

When Pentes began her junior year at Chapel Hill, she spent a lot of time with Kuralt. She urged him to run for editor of *The Daily Tar Heel*. He urged her to run for student government. Both did and won.

The two were such close friends that Kuralt's parents actually expected them to marry. But Pentes had no interest in marriage. "Everybody was fawning over Charlie," she said. "He could do everything, and he had this marvelous baritone voice. The girls were all over him."

Instead, Kuralt married Guthery when he was 19 and she was 20. Pentes thought they were too young. "It's a drastic mistake to fall in love when you're 14 and continue that, because we all change," she said. Pentes' judgment was borne out when the newlyweds moved to New York. The demands on Kuralt's time were such that he was seldom home. Guthery stayed in the Brooklyn apartment with their two baby girls. The isolation of motherhood was too much. The young couple ended their marriage over the phone. Guthery had to close down the apartment and take care of the move back to North Carolina.

"To come back home without a husband and with two young girls must just have been more than she could stand," Pentes said. "She was so conscientious, just such a good person, so I think it was extremely difficult for her."

On visits to Charlotte, Kuralt often caught up with Pentes and her husband Jack. In every setting, Kuralt dominated the conversation. In New York once to visit their son, a graduate student at NYU, Ruth and Jack caught up with Kuralt and his second wife, "Petie." They gathered for a dinner party at Kuralt's favorite Italian restaurant in Greenwich Village, The Beatrice Inn. Kuralt regaled the dinner party, which included Ruth's son and his girlfriend, with stories about his many adventures as a reporter for CBS. The next day, Pentes asked her son what his girlfriend thought of Kuralt. "She said he talks too much," the young man replied.

While in New York, Kuralt continued to write to Pentes. Occasionally they got together for lunch or dinner. Their meetings became more frequent after Kuralt left CBS. Each time Pentes and Kuralt got together, she grew more disturbed by what she saw. "I had seen Charlie over the years get fatter and fatter," she said. "I knew he drank. I knew he smoked. I knew he ate badly. We had lunch at the Four Seasons in New York one time and sat there for four hours. He drank a couple of bottles of wine just sitting there in the afternoon."

But then Kuralt drank of life. "Nothing got away from him, and that includes eating and drinking and everything you could do," Pentes said. "Had he not done all that, he wouldn't have been Charlie. You read about his month in Charleston [in *Charles Kuralt's America*], it's all about eating. So I think to have been disciplined would not have done well with him."

In his letters, Kuralt often gave the impression that he envied Pentes' settled life. "Three cats and two dogs and two children sounds pretty good to me," he wrote to her.

"But you see, he never did that," she said. "He couldn't. He wasn't meant to do that. There was no way he could have had a family. And knowing the family he came from, he probably missed it."

DECLINING HEALTH

At a Central High School reunion shortly before Kuralt's death, an exhausted Kuralt told Pentes, "I can't walk from here to that front door without sitting down and catching my breath."

Charles saw Chapel Hill as a place of freedom. While he had freedom in Charlotte, he was more like a potted plant there. Chapel Hill made him blossom. And when he could no longer be contained by the boundaries of Chapel Hill, he became a New York personality, then a national personality, then a world personality.

—C.D. Spangler,
president emeritus of UNC

Tar Heel Days

(1951–55)

When Charles Kuralt arrived in Chapel Hill, there were few issues to galvanize the student body. "I couldn't get anybody stirred up except for a few professors," said Rolfe Neill, recalling his early years as editor of The Daily Tar Heel. *"It was just a time in which whatever human tumult is always present was thoroughly hidden or draped. Students were academics only," devoid of revolutionary ideas of protest.* Time *magazine labeled theirs the "Silent Generation."*

NORTH CAROLINA COLLECTION, UNC LIBRARY AT CHAPEL HILL

Doubly Endorsed . . .
For A COMPLETE
Daily Tar Heel

UP   SP

CHARLES KURALT
FOR
DTH EDITOR

In 1954, Kuralt ran for—and won—editorship of The Daily Tar Heel. *Pro-integration, anti-McCarthy and anti-big-time sports, Kuralt adopted liberal themes during his year as editor. An FBI man appeared at the* Tar Heel *offices the morning after the paper ran an article poking fun at Sen. Joseph McCarthy. "You've ruined your lives," the FBI man announced to the staff. "Your names are going to be in the files forever." Kuralt later said he "toyed with the idea" of using the Freedom of Information Act to see if his name did indeed go into the FBI's files.*

C HARLES KURALT BEGAN his freshman year at UNC in 1951. He was only 16. His grades that first year were uneven. He did well in Spanish (surprising, given his fear back at Central High School), Air Science, Psychology and Western Civilization. He scored A's and B's in Recent British and American Poetry, Procedures and Problems of Government in the United States, and Freshman Composition. But he barely squeaked through with D's in Great Britain Since 1867, The United Nations and Air Power Concepts. He posted a B for Recreation the first semester, then slid to an "Incomplete" and a series of F's in later semesters. By the fall semester in 1954, records show only that he was "Absent" from the required Recreation course. Clearly his interests were elsewhere.

When WUNC hit the air in 1953, Kuralt was already on board as a broadcaster for the campus radio station. He did half an hour of radio drama, his

Student announcers, Kuralt and Carl Kasell, broadcasting from WUNC.

voice joining that of Carl Kasell, later of National Public Radio.

In 1954, his junior year at UNC, Kuralt ran for editor of *The Daily Tar Heel*. He printed up some posters and adopted a platform that was pro-integration, anti-McCarthy and anti-big-time sports (Kuralt opposed alumni monetary gifts to UNC athletes). His opponent for the job was the incumbent sports editor, Tom Peacock, and the campaign turned into a lively affair of clashing philosophies. Peacock took the stance that editorials should be "as conservative as the student body," while Kuralt argued that editorials should not be "mere reflections of things everybody knows. If the majority

think twice...
before you vote today.
ECIDE ON THE MOST EXPERIENCED,
BEST QUALIFIED CANDIDATE
for a finer daily tar heel:
CHARLIE KURALT...
for EDITOR • doubly endorsed

Eager for "Charlie" to win election, renegade Tar Heel *staffers slipped the insert above into the Election Eve issue of the paper. "We knew the election was going to be close," said Charles Childs of the* Tar Heel *news staff. "So we did everything we could. The flyer we inserted the night before the election probably made the difference."*

NORTH CAROLINA COLLECTION, UNC LIBRARY AT CHAPEL HILL

Flag-waving Daily Tar Heel *staffers left little doubt about who they supported. Kuralt was the hand-picked successor to Editor Rolfe Neill.*

agrees, so much the better," he said in a pre-election *Tar Heel* interview. "But editorial freedom must not be restricted by force of numbers." Kuralt stood firm in his belief that "the editorial column alone is reserved for the use of the editor, and he must not make of it a sort of Gallup Poll," Kuralt said. "It is his duty to consider all points of view and take an honest stand without respect to numbers or nature of the opposition."

The Daily Tar Heel used the occasion of April Fool's Day that year to poke fun at the two candidates. Following is the paper's lead column, headlined "Tom, Charlie Battle It Out Before Court."

Tom Peacock and Charles Kuralt both invoked the Fifth Amendment last night in a star chamber session of the Student Council as charges of "liar" filled the hall.

The candidates were up before the court for calling each

Kuralt beat his opponent, sports editor Tom Peacock, by only 226 votes.

other "Fifth Amendment Invokers." And as the trial reached its climax last night, both did invoke the controversial amendment. Special witness Joe McCarthy declared, "Both these candidates are trying to gain power of the student propaganda medium."

The visiting purger said Peacock's statement that he was "as conservative as the student body" was a "Red trick." He sharply assailed Kuralt for his big-time stand. Meantime, both Kuralt and Peacock insisted it was the Fifth Amendment of the student constitution they invoked, rather than that of the federal constitution.

Titled "The Daily Witch Hunt," the special edition featured two retouched photos of Sen. McCarthy using a magnifying glass to investigate activities of "The Horse." The caption read: "At left, McCarthy is shown as he began his investigation. When it was pointed out that 'The Eye of the Horse' was at the other end, he went around to take a look at that."

The balloting was held on April 6, and that night Kuralt posted a "Late Election Results" bulletin board near South Building on campus. Among the "returns" he listed were Malenkov (the former Russian premier) 8,739,533, Kuralt 0. But as *The Daily Tar Heel* reported the next morning, Kuralt had won the election—by a narrow margin, though, capturing only 1,585 of 2,944 votes.

The job of editor paid $30 a week, and Kuralt immediately popped the question to his girlfriend, Sory Guthery, a student at Woman's College in Greensboro. They were married the following August at Myers Park Baptist Church in Charlotte. The newlyweds moved to a cabin beside a cornfield a few miles out of Chapel Hill on the road to Raleigh. In *A Life on the Road* Kuralt wrote: "Our senior year, I remember as pure joy. We studied history and read poetry together in the morn-

The Daily Tar Heel *staff under the leadership of Kuralt, second from left in the back row. Ed Yoder Jr., standing second from right, remembered his first impression of Kuralt as a "somewhat chubby fellow, crew-cut as we all were then, with a ready smile and a voice as rich and resonant as the fine bourbon that none of us could afford to drink."*

ings; in the afternoons, I wrote my editorials, often trying them out on Sory by telephone before sending them to the printer."

Tar Heel Associate Editor Edwin M. Yoder Jr. remembered Kuralt as a collegial editor. Kuralt held strong views on issues such as integration, but he did not come off as an angry young man, Yoder said. "One of the things that always impressed me about Charlie was that he abhorred the rhetorical brutality that we see so much more of in journalism now," Yoder said. "Charlie was a very gentle man. He had a motto on his typewriter, to the effect that people don't need to always clobber one another.

"That impressed me, since my rhetorical style at that time was to blast away," Yoder added. "He taught me temperance in writing and rhetoric. And it was something that remained characteristic of his style, that gentleness and consideration and reluctance to be harsh or brutal."

Yoder also was drawn to Kuralt's enthusiasm. "Charlie was a romantic and stricken with lifelong wanderlust," Yoder said. "Everything new was a revelation for him. He had more genuine enthusiasm for novelty and interest in people and events than anyone I've ever known."

In later years, when Kuralt was with CBS News and Yoder was a Washington editor, Kuralt took his old college pal to The Players, the New York club where Shakespearean actor Edwin Booth spent the last five years of his life. The club is filled with portraits of Booth in various roles. "I recall little about the food," Yoder said. "But I recall vividly how Charlie took me from nook to cranny and from portrait to portrait, weaving his usual captivating tale out of the mere experience of being there—of imagining Booth's presence there with us."

Tar Heel Associate Editor Louis Kraar saw that same sort of enthusiasm on a road trip to Washington, D.C., during their junior year at Chapel Hill, when he and Kuralt drove all night to the nation's capital to sit in on the Army-McCarthy hearings. Both students were dead broke. Kraar had to sell his textbooks to raise cash for the trip. But once Kuralt had his mind set on something, there was no turning back.

"Charlie just drove himself when he got revved up about something," Kraar said. "He would just go on and on. He had that great energy, but no boundaries. That was both his strength and his weakness—it just wore him out. He would just go on and on with something until he would drop."

Witnessing the hearings in person was all-important to Kuralt. "We all shared a kind of liberal idealism that was very much reflected in *The Daily Tar Heel* in those days," Kraar said. "Charlie was probably the most eloquent and articulate, but we all shared the same ideal."

Those liberal ideas sometimes clashed with the conservative elements of the student body. In 1955, two members of the student legislature charged the *Tar Heel* with being a "Communist front newspaper." Kuralt called the charges "patently absurd."

The young editor adopted racial integration as a crusade. He was sickened that Frank Porter Graham, one of his mentors, had run for the U.S. Senate but lost after he was shown standing with a black person.

When the U.S. Supreme Court, in its landmark 1954 ruling *Brown vs. Board of Education*, mandated an end to school segregation, Kuralt urged North Carolina to get on with it, starting with the university. His plan of action included making sure state legislators got copies of the *Tar Heel*, which contained such editorials as the one that follows. He got noticed. On the floor of the all-white legislature, the young editor was denounced as "a pawn of the Communists."

THE DECISION

MAY 18, 1954

The Supreme Court yesterday struck a mighty blow in the American struggle for individual freedom and equality before the law.

Southern schools, this University among them, must now face the truth—that "separate but equal" is a meaningless phrase, that places of learning, if separated, are inherently unequal.

We hold this one—like those other great truths declared in our Constitution—to be self-evident: It is time to stop postponing brotherhood. This is a time for the turning of thought and opinion into wide, new channels, a time for yielding the old prejudices and ignorant discrimination before the patient and powerful light of Christianity.

Even if ethics did not compel it, the international position of the United States requires us to enter this new day in Southern education with resolution. We stand as the champion of the free world, as the protector of dignity of the minority, as men with inalienable and unassailable rights. This is lent special significance in a world in which the majority of people, by our standards, are colored.

However, it would be erroneous and immoral to predicate doing the right thing upon the wrong reason; for the practical considerations, important as they are, are none the less secondary. We hail the Supreme Court decision, not because it enhances our prestige in a troubled world, not because it pleases a segment of professional equalizers, but because it is the right thing to do.

South Carolina's Governor Byrnes and many like him in the South, many of them our friends and people we love, now stand eclipsed. Their South is gone, or it is going, and the bitterness and antagonism no longer seem very

He had a voice, and he was a better writer than all of us. He was a great storyteller. He was lyrical. But his greatest attribute was his irrepressible enthusiasm. And that was infectious. He inspired us.

—Louis Kraar, pictured

significant, though we do not deny that there is bitterness yet to be overcome before perfect equality is achieved, even in North Carolina, even in Chapel Hill. It is simply that the path is now very clear indeed, and for the Southern states and the University, there is no other path, though we be emotionally reluctant at first to follow it.

From whatever point you view it, the essential equity of the Court's verdict is plain to see. That, we think, is a good test; the human test, how you feel about it. And we feel good.

Near the end of his senior year, Kuralt left UNC to take a job with the *Charlotte News*. His graduating class walked without him. His degree in history would not be granted until 10 years later, when UNC modified graduation requirements.

In preparation for a *Daily Tar Heel* reunion in 1968, Kuralt and his former colleagues were asked to complete a questionnaire about their current jobs and their thoughts about the old days. When asked, "Have you worked any time in journalism?" the CBS News correspondent had a wry one-word answer: "Debatable."

Another question asked for reflection on their *Daily Tar Heel* experience. Kuralt wrote: "To be free to deliver oneself of opinions at the rate of three a day—to know and work with the likes of Jim Wallace, Rolfe Neill, Ed Yoder, Louis Kraar, Barry Farber, Harry Snook, Fred Powledge—obviously one of the finer, freer, more stimulating years of my life. The *DTH* taught all the lessons of journalism and some of the lessons of life—if we only had possessed the wit to learn them."

In 1987, he returned to Chapel Hill as a working journalist and dropped in on the newspaper office to have a look around. "Hello, I'm Charles Kuralt," he announced. "And he certainly was," the subsequent *Daily Tar Heel* story said.

*Kuralt did not walk with his graduating class. He was too busy editing
the student-run* Daily Tar Heel *and working in radio broadcasting to
find time for his schoolwork or to attend classes. Following Kuralt's
death in 1997, newspapers reported that the North Carolina native graduated from UNC in 1955 with a degree in journalism. Not so. He failed
to complete a couple of required physical education courses. Kuralt left
Chapel Hill in the summer of 1955 with no degree, to take a job with
the* Charlotte News. *Ten years later, the university modified graduation
requirements, allowing Kuralt to claim his degree, a bachelor of arts in
history*

More A's
Than Ever

BILL GEER
UNC History Professor

At Chapel Hill, Kuralt learned about his state and the nation under the tutelage of history professor Bill Geer. "God, I had great teachers," Kuralt said in a 1996 interview with North Carolina's *The State* magazine. "I walked into Bill Geer's class my freshman year not knowing anything. None of us knew anything. And he plunked Gunnar Myrdal's book *The American Dilemma* down on the desk and said, 'The first thing you're going to read is about race in America,' something very few of us had thought about, I assure you. And there began our education about the world."

By the time Kuralt arrived at UNC, he had already developed "a hard-nosed concern for humanity," Geer said in an interview shortly before his own death. "Charles had a remarkable mind, an extraordinary vocabulary and a resonant voice, but his sensitivity was what struck his fellow classmates and his instructors most clearly."

NORTH CAROLINA COLLECTION, UNC LIBRARY AT CHAPEL HILL

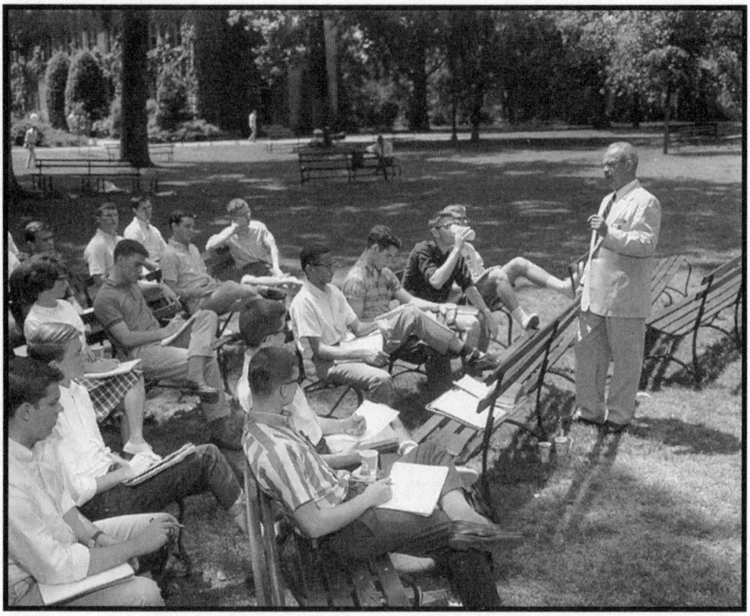

Throughout his early years, Kuralt had great teachers. Among them—Anne Batten, at Alexander Graham Junior High School, and Bill Geer, shown here teaching students on the lawn at UNC-Chapel Hill.

During the semester that he had Kuralt in his class, Geer dispensed more A's than ever before. "He was a bright man and he contributed a lot to the discussion in class," Geer said. "We disagreed from time to time, but he always added something that was interesting. He inspired other members of the class in their beliefs, and that class did exceptionally well, partly because of Charles."

Kuralt once told Geer the reason he devoted himself in the classroom was because he shared the same liberal idealism as Geer and other faculty members. "We were all liberals," Geer said. "And that appealed to him. In later years, he would say that my point of view was different from any other point of view he had experienced. Of course, I had no way to confirm that, but I was delighted."

Kuralt and Geer stayed in touch over the years. Whenever CBS assignments took him to Chapel Hill, Kuralt would call on his old professor. And whenever Geer made it to New York, he would look up his now-famous student. During one such trip, they made plans to meet for dinner at the Waldorf-Astoria, but when Geer arrived, he found a note instead, in which Kuralt apologized for standing him up. "CBS had sent him out to Kennedy Airport to meet Mr. Krushchev," Geer said. "I knew I couldn't compete with that."

The Tar Heel *was the center of life for the people who worked there.*

—Fred Powledge

Sleepyhead

FRED POWLEDGE
Daily Tar Heel *News Staff*

S OME EDITORS OF *THE DAILY TAR HEEL* immersed themselves in the job, overseeing every aspect of the newspaper's production. Others were much more hands-off, and Kuralt fell into that category. "A lot of us enjoyed the mechanics of the paper, going to the print shop after the paper was made up and getting our hands dirty with ink," said staffer Fred Powledge. "Charles was more of an intellectual editor. He was responsible for some really excellent writing in the *Tar Heel*."

Kuralt and Powledge were more than just colleagues on the paper. They lived in the same boardinghouse, on Henderson Street in Chapel Hill. Powledge's room was in the basement, Kuralt's a couple of floors above. Each morning, Powledge would walk upstairs to rouse Kuralt.

"He was incapable of waking up in the morning," Powledge said. "Very often, I would be the one who turned off his alarm clock, which was ringing right beside his head.

[Upon first meeting Kuralt] I was first struck by how articulate he was. He knew how to talk, possibly as a result of having worked in radio but also I think as a result of coming from a family that enjoyed learning things. He could converse with professors better than any other student I knew. It was sort of as if he were on their level, and he probably was.

—Fred Powledge

He could only wake up if somebody said, 'Charlie, it's late. You're going to be late for class, and they're going to kick you out of school.'"

On days when Kuralt could get moving fast enough, he and Powledge would shuffle down to Franklin Street for breakfast at the UNC cafeteria. They nearly always talked shop. A new dean had just come to the School of Journalism and wanted the *Tar Heel* to become a laboratory newspaper for journalism students. "We were utterly disdainful of the journalism school," Powledge said. "And so we told the new dean, 'In your dreams,' or whatever the expression might have been in those days."

Besides, the *Tar Heel* staff barely had time for writing, editing and producing the paper. Allowing the School of Journalism to meddle in the paper's affairs would have only increased the burden on the staff.

"It was a struggle between putting out the *Tar Heel* and doing what we were supposed to be doing—going to classes and doing what the professor said and writing papers and passing those classes and moving on to the next level," Powledge added. "The *Tar Heel* took a tremendous amount of time, probably because it was published so frequently. It might as well have been a seven-day-a-week paper, because with just one full day off, you never had time to catch up."

PERSPECTIVE

Charles was assigned to do a story on a parade. And so instead of just going down there and taking pictures and describing the parade, he saw this little kid and got down on his knees and did a story from the kid's perspective.

—Richard Cole, dean of UNC School of Journalism

Most people would pass by the bum on the street and not give him a second thought. But to Charlie, that person was a story. Charlie could draw something out of that person. He captured the essence of people and presented it in a fascinating way.

—Ken Sanford

Sir Charles

KEN SANFORD
Daily Tar Heel *News Staff*

T WO STORIES KURALT WROTE FOR THE *Tar Heel* convinced Ken Sanford that here was someone destined for greatness. The first revolved around a series of firings within the Baptist State Convention. The *Tar Heel* had learned that a Baptist committee investigating liberalism was giving the campus ministers at UNC and Duke University the opportunity to resign or be fired. Before confirming the story, the *Tar Heel* staff sent news of the reported firings over the news wire.

"The dailies started calling us, but we still hadn't verified the story," Sanford said. "We knew the decision was to be made by the board of the Baptist State Convention, so Charles went down a list of about 100 people and started calling them. One after the other, they said they couldn't comment. Then one person confirmed the story. So we broke a major story that was picked up on the front pages across the state. We were impressed with Charles for getting that story."

Ken Sanford, center, with Kuralt and printer J.B. Holland, right, review
The Daily Tar Heel *hot off the press.*

The other story concerned a young man, Charles Childs, who met a girl from Woman's College in Greensboro but let her get away without learning her name. All he knew was that she wore a yellow raincoat. So he put an ad in *The Carolinian*, the student paper in Greensboro, hoping the girl would see it and contact him.

Kuralt interviewed the hapless student and made a great tale of his woe, characterizing him in the story as Sir Charles seeking his fair maiden. Kuralt's story began:

> *This is the story of a twentieth century knight-errant, a tale of mystery and high adventure, set on the Carolina campus. Our knight (he lives in 312 Joyner dormitory) is named Charlie Childs—Sir Charles for the purposes of our story— and like all knights worthy of the title, he's on a quest. Such everyday goals as the Holy Grail, however, hold no interest for him. His is a quest for a damsel, a Woman's College maiden clothed in yellow.*

Kuralt's "Sir Charles" saga, which appeared as a series in *The Daily Tar Heel*, represented his first byline in the paper. Sanford recalled that the series made "quite a stir" on campus, engaging readers in the young man's plight. Despite Kuralt's efforts, however, Childs did not succeed in finding the elusive fair maiden.

VOICE APPEAL

Kuralt's voice alone was enough to recruit one *Tar Heel* staffer. "Babbie Jane DiIorio was totally fascinated by his voice," said Ken Sanford. "His voice did give him a commanding presence."

He was one of the best storytellers the world has ever known. He became very popular on the air while working for WBT, and that's the reason I recommended him to CBS.

—Charles Crutchfield

Projecting Voice

CHARLES CRUTCHFIELD

President, Jefferson Pilot Communications

D URING HIS COLLEGE YEARS, Kuralt spent summers working for Charlotte's WBT and WBTV, former CBS affiliates that were acquired by Jefferson Pilot Communications. One of his first jobs there was announcing a radio program called "Men Who Make Music," an award-winning production of the Davidson College Orchestra and Glee Club. He became very popular on the air and made a strong impression on Jefferson Pilot President Charles Crutchfield. The WBT executive not only hired Kuralt the following summers but also recommended that CBS, headed by his good friend and CBS President Bill Paley, take a look at him.

"He was just a bright, brilliant young man," Crutchfield said a few months before his own death. "He noticed everything, and he knew how to describe it in everyday conversation. He was really a master at it. He hadn't had any formal training at all. It just came natural to him."

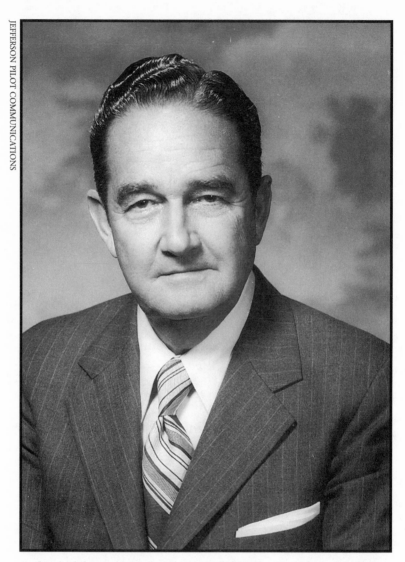

As head of the company that owned WBT Radio, Charles Crutchfield recommended to his friends at CBS that they take a look at WBT's young new anchor, Charles Kuralt.

Kuralt occasionally appeared in front of the camera to do a commercial for WBTV. He later said he would have gone to work for WBT after college "if they would have had much of a news department, but in 1955, they didn't. It was just Nelson Benton and a handful of others, so I didn't even apply."

He went to work instead for the *Charlotte News*. To his surprise, though, he found Nelson was beating "us professional reporters," to the odd story. "It softened my contempt for broadcast journalists, who I thought were (and who mostly were) just announcers then," Kuralt later said.

On the air, Kuralt's style was akin to that of Edward R. Murrow and Eric Sevareid, Crutchfield added. "He had body language, mostly through his mouth and eyes," Crutchfield recalled. "You knew he was sincere. His images were perfect when he described anything. And never once did you hear Charlie talk about himself on those programs, which is unlike most radio announcers. I know. I used to be one, and it's pretty difficult not to give your own opinion about things. But he didn't do that."

Among Tom Spain's sharpest memories of Kuralt was his enthusiasm for debating politics. "He was working as a waiter at St. Anthony Hall, and he was talking real loud about Adlai Stevenson," Spain said. "I couldn't understand why all these guys were arguing about the merits of Eisenhower versus Stevenson. Kuralt was really impassioned. It impressed me that he cared so much about the politics and the election that was coming up."

Frat Brothers

TOM SPAIN
College Pal and CBS Colleague

I N HIS SOPHOMORE YEAR, Kuralt was invited to join St.
Anthony Hall, a literary fraternity located near the
Carolina Inn, and there he met Tom Spain. The two struck
up a friendship that lasted to the day of Kuralt's death.

Both were interested in radio. By the time Kuralt came to
UNC, he was already a veteran broadcaster, having passed
time at WAYS in Charlotte. "In those days, being a radio
announcer was a pretty prestigious thing," Spain said,
"because radio was bigger, way bigger, than television."

Summers during college, Kuralt worked for Charlotte's
WBT. There, he began to gain national recognition. Hugh
Holder, a CBS staff announcer who owned several radio sta-
tions in North Carolina, occasionally called Kuralt and asked
him to join CBS. Holder gained his own measure of broadcasting fame as the voice introducing the TV show, "The Lone
Ranger." "A fiery horse with the speed of light, a cloud of dust
and a hearty, 'Hi yo Silver.'"

Tom Spain remembers Holder calling Kuralt "on that funny old telephone in the back room of the fraternity house. He would tell him there was a job opening and that he ought to quit college and come to New York."

Perhaps what stopped Kuralt from accepting were the words of his hero, Edward R. Murrow. Shortly before Kuralt graduated high school, he met the celebrated CBS broadcaster in Chapel Hill. In a letter to friend Wesley Wallace years later, Kuralt wrote of meeting Murrow: "Awed. Heart beat faster; there he was in the same room." Kuralt accompanied Murrow and a driver to the airport. On the way, the veteran broadcaster counseled Kuralt to establish himself first as a print journalist before moving to broadcast news.

But it was clear that Kuralt was preparing for a career in broadcasting. He made a point of listening nightly to the "CBS News Roundup," and began imitating the reporting styles of Murrow and Eric Sevareid. "He really admired those guys," Spain said. "He would say, 'This is CBS,' and he would smoke Pall Mall cigarettes the way Murrow did. Even when I was in the hospital there visiting him [during the days before Kuralt died], he would quote the Pall Mall radio announcer who said, 'Fully packed, and they are mild.' He memorized all that stuff."

Occasionally during college holidays, Kuralt visited his friend Spain in New Jersey, and they drove Spain's 1947

THE OLD GRUB

Kuralt was so untidy that his fraternity brothers amiably took to calling him "the old grub." His clothes were generally rumpled, he was a tad overweight, and he usually needed a shave, recalled roommate David Clinard.

Ford into New York. Their usual ports of call were jazz clubs and The Strand bookstore. During one trip, they also made a call on CBS headquarters. Kuralt went in to talk with some of the correspondents, while Spain waited outside in the car. Kuralt was already establishing rapport with the people he would later work with.

Weekends back in Chapel Hill, Kuralt begged Spain for his car so he could travel to Greensboro to date sweetheart Sory Guthery, and after the couple married, Kuralt talked Spain into getting wed as well. "It sounded so wonderful and romantic," Spain said. "They were going to live in Joe Phillips' old farmhouse on the outskirts of town. And so I married the girl I was dating and moved to another farmhouse on the north end of town. We hung out together during those last years of school."

In his senior year, Kuralt went back to Charlotte to take a job with the *Charlotte News,* and Spain returned to New Jersey. One March afternoon in 1957, Kuralt called Spain with the news that he had accepted a job at CBS and was moving to New York. Spain opened his home to his college buddy while he hunted for a place to live.

Kuralt eventually found an apartment in an old house on Brooklyn's Middagh Street. In *A Life on the Road*, he painted a vivid picture of that apartment and his new neighbors.

The paint was peeling off the walls a little bit, but the kitchen afforded a partial view of the Brooklyn Bridge and the Manhattan towers. Downstairs lived a dour modern artist named Charles Duback. Upstairs lived a jovial folk singer, Lee Hays of The Weavers quartet, blacklisted and unable to find employment because of alleged left-wing associations in his peripatetic past. Duback worked below, creating vast geometric canvases nobody wanted to buy. Lee

In 1963, Nevada State Penitentiary's warden invited Kuralt, Tom Spain, Irv Drasnin, a producer for the CBS Evening News, and cameraman Jerry Sims to film a documentary about Synanon, a drug rehabilitation program based on "tough love" and peer-group support. Pictured across from Kuralt is Synanon group leader Candy Latson.

Hays worked above, composing songs on his guitar that
nobody wanted to listen to. I was the only person in the
house who ever put on a necktie and went to work, which
sort of ruined the Bohemian style of the place.

Eager always to keep himself busy, Kuralt began looking for
ways to earn extra money in New York. Spain was able to throw
some work his way. Spain had landed a job working for a man
who produced industrial films, and they needed someone who
could write scripts. "We would struggle and work hard to get
these narrations about, say, how Corning makes glass and that
sort of thing," Spain said. "We would spend weeks and days
trying to get every word just right and wondering whether it
was OK. And Charles would come in and just bang, bang,
bang—it was done. I remember the boss was so impressed with
this kid who could come in and knock out these little scripts
without agonizing over them like we did."

Later, Spain himself landed a job at CBS. He was in the

THE MASTER OF MONOLOGUE

In later years, Kuralt and Tom Spain worked together
on a documentary about the famous composer John
Philip Sousa. Spain's film featured a 26-year-old self-
trained scholar who had discovered stories about Sousa
in the basement of the Library of Congress. Spain ran
the film once for Kuralt, and then they took a cab
across town to the studio where the broadcaster was to
record the narration. On the way, Kuralt sighed, "God,
I wish I could tell a story like that kid." He then proceeded to recite, verbatim, the entire monologue from
the film, "with the right rhythms and everything,"
Spain said. "It was wonderful."

cafeteria for coffee one morning when Kuralt walked up and said, "What are you doing here?" Spain replied, "I work here." Kuralt said, "Well," and they immediately started working on projects together.

One such project was a documentary about Synanon, a drug rehabilitation program based on "tough love" and peer-group support. Nevada State Penitentiary had a good program, and in 1963 the warden invited Kuralt, Irv Drasnin, a producer for the CBS Evening News, and cameraman Jerry Sims to film some of the sessions.

"This was before television was really all that rich with those kind of documentaries," Spain said. "It was beautifully photographed, and they shot these wonderful sessions with these criminals, killers, gamblers and drug addicts who were trying to sort out their lives. They brought it back to CBS, and someone there said, 'That's interesting, but what's the news peg?' And so they never ran it."

But Kuralt knew it was good, so he held onto the film. When he discovered Spain was working for a documentary unit called "The Twentieth Century," Kuralt saw a chance to use the film to leverage his way out of his news rut. "And so we conspired to take some of this material and show it to the boss of our unit," Spain said. "I worked on it for a few days to put up a pitch reel. We showed it to the boss, and he liked it. He commissioned Kuralt and Irv and me to make a half-hour show out of it."

The trio set out to update and supplement the existing footage. Spain remembers it as a fun trip, and a lavish one, too. They ate well and stayed in the best hotels. "I remember thinking this was the guy who taught me all of this populist stuff about the Democrats and the people, and here we were hanging around all the swells," Spain recalled, laughing. "But I think he was always that way. That's why he was in the fraternity we were in, because it was kind of elite. He lived very well, and he really aspired to that."

Kuralt also aspired to live very much alone, not squandering his private self. "I don't think anybody spent more than 36 hours with him," Spain said. "I've been with him on islands in Alaska out in the Bering Sea, where you can't get out, and you get into the second or third day, and he really started to sweat."

Spain visited with Kuralt at the hospital the day before he died. They spent time mapping out their next project. "He was going to appear in a documentary I was doing about America in the '40s, and we were scheduled to shoot with him on July 15," Spain said. "I spent half a day with him there. We had a wonderful time. He was recovering. He was very enthused. He'd not been well at all the week before. I was doubtful if he was going to make it, but on July 3, he looked great. We were talking about doing the work just a week ahead. And then I got a call the next day that he was gone."

SMOKE, SMOKE, SMOKE THAT CIGARETTE

Charles was devoted to cigarettes. He wouldn't have called it an addiction. He once said that should a doctor one day tell him he had lung cancer and only six months to live he might feel a twinge of regret but until then he enjoyed it too much to quit. Only a couple of days after his heart surgery we were alone in his hospital room when he furtively looked toward the corridor and said: "Will you find my cigarettes? They're around here somewhere." I stared back in disbelief. He persisted. I refused. He pleaded. I pretended to look, telling him I couldn't find them. He pointed to where I had not looked. I stood my ground. He insisted. "Only one, I swear it." He prevailed. "Now," he said, holding the cigarette, "do me a favor and turn off the oxygen before I light the match."

—Irv Drasnin, former CBS News producer

When I finally went to work for my hometown newspaper, my folks were still very helpful to me. I think my mother had more doubts about my being a reporter than my father did. My father was in the press all the time, trying to keep the county commission from cutting welfare benefits to poor children, and all that kind of thing. And it was a conservative community, so he was on the hot seat constantly, at war with the county commissioners. And my newspaper editorially sometimes supported the other side. My mother, at least twice, canceled our family's subscription to the newspaper I was working on, because she was so mad about its treatment of my father.

—Charles Kuralt in 1996 interview with the Academy of Achievement

"People"

(1955-57)

ALMOST A YEAR AFTER HE AND SORY MARRIED, Kuralt left UNC short of graduation and moved with his bride to Charlotte, where he took a full-time job as a reporter. The job was with the *Charlotte News*, the paper whose sports-writing contests he entered as a teenager not so many years before. Pay was $55 a week.

As the largest evening paper in the two Carolinas, the *News* was considered a writer's newspaper and despite a small staff had produced a sizable number of noted journalists. Alumni included Harry Ashmore, a Pulitzer Prize winner; Marion Hargrove, author of the World War II bestseller *See Here, Private Hargrove*; the historian Burke Davis; and W.J. Cash, who penned *The Mind of the South*, one of the most celebrated books ever written about the South.

The reporters were a scrappy and competitive lot. "Our goal," Kuralt said in an interview later in life, "was to leave nothing for the morning paper to report on."

In his "On the Road" series years later, Kuralt would seek out the same sort of people and the same types of stories he specialized in at the Charlotte News. *"That tells you where his mind was," said* News *colleague Julian Scheer, above. "He was continually interested in people, had a great empathy for people, and it was a feeling from day one that 'I can write about people interestingly because they interest me, and they should interest you, and they don't have to be celebrities.' They are people he thought you'd feel glad to know about."*

Editorially more liberal than many papers in the South, the *News* provided a nurturing environment for aspiring young writers like Kuralt.

He began as a general assignment reporter and assumed he would work his way up the ladder to become the paper's star reporter or perhaps an editorial writer. Among his early assignments: a lead article about Vicki, a circus elephant who escaped and eluded capture in Mecklenburg County for 11 days; and a story about a Charlotte bridegroom who opened an airliner door and hurtled 6,500 feet to his death.

Kuralt also covered city politics and election stories. But it did not take long for him to learn that hard news reporting was not going to be his forte. That became plain the day he was assigned to write about prostitution in Charlotte.

Julian Scheer, who worked with Kuralt at the *News*, said the assignment was a test to see how much digging the young reporter would do. "Charles jumped right into it and started calling people—policemen, his contacts at City Hall and people who lived in the neighborhoods where the hookers may have lived. He reported back that there wasn't really any prostitution in Charlotte."

The managing editor promptly called Kuralt into his office and also pulled Scheer in, saying: "Charles says we don't have prostitutes in this town. Is that right, Julian?" Scheer replied that he thought there might be a few. "Well," the editor grumbled, "can you get one on the phone so Charles can talk to her?"

Kuralt was downcast, feeling he had done a bad job, but Scheer cheered him up. "I just said, 'Charles, don't worry about it. It ain't an overwhelming population that you have to worry about in Charlotte. And business is not too good for hookers in this town.' And he laughed and that was the end of it."

In 1957, Kuralt received the Ernie Pyle Memorial Award for his "People" columns. The award included a $1,000 check, presented by News Managing Editor Dick Young. The award also caught the attention of CBS. A few months after this photo, Kuralt was off to New York to begin a career with the network giant that spanned almost four decades.

But it hardened his friend's resolve to go after stories more aggressively, Scheer said. "He would get some crummy assignments, but to him it was an assignment and he was going to get something in the paper, and that had great meaning for him."

Fate stepped in one day when Managing Editor Tom Fesperman tapped him to write a column called "People."

In 1957, after only a year at the *News*, Kuralt won the Ernie Pyle Memorial Award for his "People" columns. Human interest, warmth and a faculty for telling a story ranked high in the judging for this prestigious award. Kuralt combined those gifts with the ability to see his stories from unusual angles. In his story about a Soap Box Derby contest, it was not the boy who won that Kuralt focused on, but the boy who lost.

WITH LUMP IN THROAT, GUS PLANS FOR FUTURE

If losing the Soap Box Derby sounds like only a minor league tragedy to you, that just shows how old you are. There's only one winner, and it wasn't Gustevas Roberts.

Gus was the last Charlotte boy eliminated.

He won his first heat and his second heat, and that put him into the quarterfinals, and he won that, too.

Then, with only four boys left in his class, and only two races away from the gold trophy and the trip to Akron, Gus Roberts lost.

A dozen other boys crowded around him before his car stopped, and they said, "Don't feel bad, Gus," and "You did fine, Gus," the way boys seek awkwardly to comfort one another.

Gustevas Roberts climbed out of his car and watched while they loaded Tony Osborn's racer on to a truck for the trip back to the top of the raceway and the championship hat.

News *photographer Tom Franklin occasionally worked with Kuralt, but as a rule the reporter preferred to go solo and take his own pictures. "He wouldn't let a photographer go with him because he thought he could get closer to the people without a third party along," Franklin said. "He was a good photographer in his own right." Some days, all it took for Kuralt to come up with a column was to walk downtown and sit on a park bench. On one occasion he dressed as a bum, above, and checked into a homeless shelter.*

A few minutes later, he stood on the edge of the crowd and watched Val Hawkins, the champion, being interviewed on the radio.

"I tried real hard," he said. "The other boy's wheels were broken in better. I worked on mine for three months, but he worked on his for four months."

They were a busy three months, with advice from his mother, and from Dr. Russell, a dentist in his Brevard St. neighborhood, and from his buddy, Isaiah.

They were a three months spent on balancing and laminating and polishing, and hoping. And they ended up with Gustevas Roberts on the edge of the crowd.

"My first year, I lost in my first heat and last year I lost in my second heat," Gus Roberts said.

He looked over at his car, the one he spent three months on.

"I've got one more year," he said. "I'm going to build another one. It's going to be better."

There was a lump in his throat.

"I'm going to start tomorrow," he said.

To Scheer, part of the magic of Kuralt's stories was that they had no spin. They were simply stories about people he thought readers would want to read about. "He took people who would be considered nobodies by most people and made them somebodies," Scheer said. "It was like, 'You should know about this person because you passed him on the street and he has an interesting story to tell. He's in our midst. He's part of the fabric of our lives.'"

WITH BACKYARD AS STAGE, JOHN GIVES CONCERT FOR YOUNGSTERS

You could hear the music way up on Morehead St.

PEOPLE

The Faces Of Freedom

BY CHARLES KURALT

Who can forget the face of a free man?

From Hungary, we have seen such faces of late. The wirephoto process has transmitted their hope and their agony across the miles—from the men dying for freedom in the streets of Budapest to the neat neighborhoods of America, from which other men have gone forth to die for freedom, and will again.

The wrinkled face of a machine-gunned Hungarian patriot is not unlike the wrinkled face of a Huntersville farmer preparing to drop a ballot in a ballot box on an American election day.

There is a kinship. And who can forget such a face?

QUIET CAME yesterday to both Hungary and Huntersville. For the patriot, it meant his desperate, hopeless revolution had been crushed. For the farmer, it meant that the tumult and the shouting of an American election was over; that it was time to vote.

Two such different meanings were born, however, of the same idea. It is not an easy idea to express. Perhaps neither the patriot nor the farmer could express it.

But they feel it, they know it, both of them.

It has to do with such names as Jefferson and Mindszenty, Yankee and Magyar, Lexington and Budapest, with such tools as rifles and newspapers and pulpits and ballot boxes.

BOTH OF THEM understand that.

Both of them—the Huntersville farmer who voted with his aged mother yesterday, and the Hungarian street fighter who lost his last battle yesterday—were thinking about it.

This is the thing that transcends the result of the American election and the failure of the Hungarian revolution.

This is the thing you could read in their faces.

And once having seen a face, who can forget it?

Kuralt

(News Staff Photo by Tom Franklin—Hunter)

THE VOTERS: Who Can Forget?

Throughout his career, Kuralt was interested in what the "little people" had to say, whether they were farmers or immigrants, above, or molasses makers, left. "He had a talent for stories about little people," said Charlotte News *Managing Editor Tom Fesperman. "And I suppose he always did stories about little people, whether it was at the* News *or later at CBS. He carried on with that style of reporting all through his career."*

It was coming from an amplified guitar in the hands of a man standing in a Vance St. backyard.

He had a big crowd around him, mostly youngsters. There was a woman washing clothes on the porch, and two men leaning against a house tapping time with their toes, and one old man sitting in his second-floor window, reading a newspaper and listening.

But the rest were boys and girls, standing in a big semi-circle. One boy, six or seven years old, sat on the guitar loudspeaker, feeling the vibrations and grinning.

The guitar player was John Honeycutt. His music drifted through the rows of houses and the crowd got bigger.

"It's like this every time I play," he said. "I just do it for the kids around here."

John Honeycutt has a four-piece band. Tuesday nights, he plays at the Zanzibar, Thursday nights at the Vet's Club, weekends he plays for dances and parties.

In the afternoon, he plays for the kids.

"The way it happened," he said, "some of 'em started pestering me to play for 'em one day. They hadn't ever heard any music except on the radio and records. I wasn't doing anything else, so I figured I might as well."

John Honeycutt had never heard music, either, when he was growing up. He had learned how to play the guitar from a 50-cent book. He bought the book before he bought the guitar.

"I would have given anything to have somebody play me music. You know how it is," he said. "It's nothing much."

That's right, it's nothing much.

To anybody but the kids.

Kuralt wrote the way he was, Scheer said, a decent, gentle

Kuralt's relationship with the Charlotte News *started when he was still a junior high school student. By age 13, he was already a celebrity, locally at least.*

CHRISTMAS AT HALF-TIME. When the Charlotte Clippers play the Quincey, Mass., Manets tomorrow in Memorial Stadium for the News Empty Stocking Fund, Charles Kuralt, above, student at Alexander Graham Jr. Hugh School, will be on hand to take part in the special Christmas program to be presented during the half - time. He will ride with Santa Claus on the field and tell his audience of "A Night Before Christmas."

person devoid of sarcasm or cynicism. Kuralt had a heightened sensitivity toward people and events and was also "very much a man of seasons," Scheer said. "If it snowed, snow had meaning to him. If it was raining, rain had meaning to him."

THE GOVERNOR'S NO CARUSO,
BUT HE'S PROUD OF HIS VOCAL CORDS

Every man has something he's proud of. With the Governor, it's his lungs.

He's got a larynx like a desert horn and a 13-year-old song that goes: "HEY, getcha Charlotte News *final eDITion PAPer today here!"*

If you've passed Thacker's in the middle of the day, you know the Governor. If you happen to be a pretty girl, you're likely to know him very well.

With the men, the Governor plays it dignified: "Paper today, sir!"

The girls get softened up: "You look like you've been down to Myrtle Beach, honey pie."

"Thank you," one answers.

"You're welcome as the flowers in June," the Governor says. "Paper?"

The Governor's name is Eugene Broughton, no relation to the late J. Melville, and he's been selling the News *in front of Thacker's ever since he left the farm at Garner to see the bright lights.*

He begins at 11 a.m. when the first edition is off the press—"I'm the first man to Tryon St. with those papers. Boy, I trot right along"—and he doesn't quit until eight o'clock, with the pink final down at the bus station.

He wears an ancient felt hat and keeps his Adam's apple hopping. You can't sell papers sitting down, boy, and you can't sell papers without talking it up."

He yanks his papers out of the stack under his arm with a pop.

"You got to show some enthusiasm, boy. I sell about 290 a day. When there's a murder, I sell maybe 320. I started out hollering right from the beginning, and the only day I ever had a sore throat was the second day, way back during the war."

The Governor is essentially a modest guy.

"I don't like to brag," he says. "But I really do believe I can out holler most people."

He takes you by the arm.

"See how far it is from here to the Liberty Life Building?" he asks.

It's pretty far.

"Well, one time a fellow who works at that radio station up there told me he was standing at the window and he heard me way down here and he could hear what I was saying."

Every man has something he's proud of.

With the Governor, that's it.

ED BENNETT'S DREAMS
SHAPED LIKE ORANGES

If he had stayed away from the plant nursery in Florida, chances are it never would have happened.

But as it was, what could Ed Bennett do?

He visited the nursery with his brother and sister-in-law to see about buying some shrubs and there were the orange trees, dozens of them, barely two feet tall.

It had been a long time since he had seen little ones like that. He thought back 39 years, back to the time he left his father's orange grove between Lakeland and Plant City to make his living elsewhere.

As a Western Union telegrapher, he had been back to Florida many times, he had seen many orange trees, but the little ones with oranges the size of golf balls. ...

He found himself reaching into his pocket and paying the man $6.50 for an orange tree. He put it in his car, and he brought it back to Charlotte. He put it in his backyard at 2413 E. 5th St.

It's still small enough to put in the basement on the chilly days. When it gets too large for that, Ed Bennett is going to build a shelter for it next to his garage. He's going to keep the shelter warm with canned heat. He's going to keep that orange tree going.

All the neighbors have come to see it.

"I think they're doubtful about the whole thing," Mr. Bennett admits.

His wife has her doubts too.

"She says I'm making a fool of myself," Mr. Bennett confesses.

But who could agree with a judgment like that? What man doesn't have an orange tree, or some kind of dream tucked in his aspirations?

Climate and temperature at 2413 E. 5th St. do not lend themselves to the cultivation of orange trees. But climate and temperature, you see, have nothing to do with it.

BE IT IN CHARLOTTE OR CHICAGO, PEOPLE CONTINUE TO BE PEOPLE

You can never get away from business, even on vacation, if your business is noticing people and writing about them.

The people are everywhere.

In Hot Springs, N.C., you glance into the face of a bearded man picking wildflowers by the highway. It bears a remarkable resemblance to the bearded face of an Amish citizen walking along Michigan Ave. in Chicago.

The simple calico dress of a blonde girl sitting on a porch near Newport, Tenn., contrasts hardly at all with the simple cotton frock of a blonde girl sitting on her porch in Sheboygan, Wis., and their tresses reflect the same amount of sunlight.

The hotel doormen in Lexington, Ky., and Evanston, Il., make the same remark: "Charlotte, N.C.? That's where Billy Graham's from, ain't it?"

Whenever you get a chance to stop and talk, the people are willing.

The publicist of the posh Shore Drive Motel, you find out, used to be a baker.

The soft-spoken owner of Clark Street's famous jazz mecca, the Blue Note, was an iron-worker, then an attendant in a mental hospital, then a railroad man.

The manager of the Sheraton-Blackstone Hotel, where the nation's Democratic Party brass will stay for the Democratic convention in August, is a Vermont farmer's son and was, and is, a Republican.

Sarah Vaughan, the bold singer of songs, is a shy and quiet girl who is scared by audiences.

Rogers Hornsby, the Hall of Fame ballplayer, spends his afternoons nowadays hitting fungos to the kids in Jackson Park. You discover things about people whose names you don't know, too.

The farmers along the Wabash and Ohio Rivers, you discover, answer the same disaster in the same way. Both rivers flooded the week before last and drowned the young corn. The farmers went to work last week replanting it— both in Indiana and Ohio.

The people are hard to hold down, just as they are in Charlotte.

You pass a trailer with a pine tree limb buckled to it—a shade tree going 55 miles per hour.

You pass a maple tree, a courageous five feet tall, just planted in Chicago's south side slum clearance project, Lake Meadows, and the only tree on the block.

You still do not know, of course, what motivated an iron-worker to want to own a jazz emporium, what brought tired old Rogers Hornsby back to the sandlots he started from, what made a resettled Negro decide he must have a maple tree.

But even not knowing these things, you can look into the faces of some of America's people and find justification for repeating an old truth, just for the record.

The good people do not live only on Trade and Tryon Sts. They live also on Wacker Dr. in Chicago and on Main St. in Hurricane, W. Va.

The good people are everywhere.

THE STRANGER AT THE STATION
WAS SEARCHING—BUT FOR WHAT?

It wasn't one of those "Pardon me, sir, but could you spare a dime" things at all. It was more of a conversation in the sun beside the Southern station, more of a monologue, really.

He leaned the stump of his leg that wasn't there against the grip of one of his crutches and pivoted back and forth one time so that he could look both ways down the tracks.

"It's a hot day, mate," he said.

His voice was a stopper, a voice you couldn't just say, "It sure is," to and go your way.

"I left the Windy City on July the fifth, and I got here July the seventh," he said, as if it were the next logical thing to say. "I have been looking this whole day for a maiden aunt of mine who lives in this city. I haven't seen her since

nineteen and forty-three."

His eyes were bloodstained brown, not red, and his chin had a tough stubble on it.

"I'm not from here, mate. I did work here for seven years in a grocery store when I was nothing but a kid, and I have been looking for that grocery store just casually, you know, and I can't even find it.

"No, I was born and brought up in Baltimore, Maryland. I was on the West Coast last month, out there at the Golden Gate, and I am going back there just as soon as I can. You know, people out there know how to live."

He moved over a few feet, under the shade of a long shed beside the tracks. He took off his old felt hat and wiped the sweat off his head.

"Aw, I don't know," he said. "Mate, I just don't know. If I could find my aunt, I might settle down here for a while, but I'm beginning to think I ain't ever going to find her.

"As a matter of fact, I don't know what I'm going to do next. You ever come into a situation like that? There are damn few places I haven't been ...

"I was in the Ninety-Second Division during the war, and I have a few friends here and there. I ran into one of them out there on the West Coast, and he didn't even give me the time of day.

"And I'll tell you something else mate. I was going to try to hit you for a sandwich, but I'll tell you what: To hell with it." *He dropped the stump of his leg down and grabbed the grip of his crutch and swung himself away across the parking lot. "Just to hell with it," he said.*

He went around the corner toward the Square, as if his maiden aunt might be in that direction, looking for a sandwich or a ticket to the Golden Gate, looking for a grocery store. Looking for something, anyway.

After Kuralt joined CBS, Scheer saw his old friend time and again. "And despite his later celebrity, he never changed," Scheer said. "As a personality, I think he sort of stood still. Success never seemed to have spoiled him or given him the proverbial big head. If he was your friend 20 years ago, he was still your friend 20 years later.

"There were tough years when CBS sent him out to exile [to South America], and people don't talk much about that," Scheer said. "He had almost instant fame and then dropped off the scope, and he struggled back up the ladder. But as I saw him off and on, even with long gaps between all those years, we picked up as if we had seen each other the day before."

In 1995, when I saw Charlie for the first time in many years, I was shocked. He had gained weight and was drinking and smoking, clearly enjoying himself. Somehow we got on the subject of health nuts, and he said there were only two kinds of people he did not like—one was the kind always telling ethnic jokes, the other was these health cops.

—Erwin Potts

PHONE SHARING

Erwin Potts and Kuralt were pals since junior high, and Potts was already working at the *News* when Kuralt came on board. The two worked side by side and often lunched together. Even during the breaks away from the newsroom, Kuralt talked about newspaper work. "He liked to have a good time, but his idea of a good time was talking about newspapers and journalism more than anything else," Potts said.

Times were tough for the *News*, which had to marshal all of its resources to keep pace with the *Observer*. "The paper could only afford one telephone for Charlie and me," Potts said. "And we were arm wrestling for it constantly."

Eventually, Potts left the *News* to join the Marines but kept in touch with his old buddy. "One of the remarkable things about him was that he really covered a lot of controversial stories, but there was no meanness in him," Potts said. "There's no way you couldn't like the guy." After Potts' stint in the Marines was up in 1958, Kuralt helped steer him to a job at the *Miami Herald*, where Kuralt had turned down a job before being grabbed by CBS.

That CBS hired Kuralt in 1957 did not surprise Potts. "He was no matinee idol, like some of the more recent anchor people," Potts said. "But he was one of those rare combinations of a guy who could write well and present himself well speaking, and so television was a natural for him."

When Kuralt was based in South America for CBS News, he sometimes would tip off the local UPI correspondent after filing a story with New York. The guy would run out and cover this story, it would hit the wire, CBS would see it in New York and say, "Oh my God. We've got to get Kuralt on that." And they'd call him up and he'd say, "It's on the way."

—Foster Davis
Former CBS News Correspondent

The CBS Years

(1957-94)

KURALT'S JOB AT CBS DID NOT MATERIALIZE exactly the way he said it did in *A Life on the Road*. He wrote that CBS called him with a job offer, and that was true—but only after he had planted the idea.

The scenario played out after Kuralt won the Ernie Pyle Memorial Award for his *Charlotte News* "People" column and CBS sent a letter of congratulations. Boldly, he seized the moment, writing back, "If you really mean you're impressed by this, isn't there something you could do?"

The ploy worked. One March afternoon in 1957 the director of news at CBS called. Did Kuralt have any interest in writing for WCBS radio news? The answer, of course, was yes.

CBS paid Kuralt's way to New York, and when he walked into the old newsroom at 485 Madison Avenue, on the 17th floor, he knew he was home. There stood his journalistic mentor, Edward R. Murrow. As he wrote in a letter to friend Wesley Wallace: "There he was again, wearing suspenders,

Kuralt's writing talent was quickly recognized. Within six months of joining CBS, he was promoted from radio to television, where he would remain for the next 37 years.

rolling up copy on the AP machine, Murrow. Awed, as before."

CBS offered Kuralt $135 a week to work the midnight to 8 a.m. shift. He confided to Wesley Wallace that he "would have paid them just to work in the same room with Murrow."

With their first baby, 1-year-old Lisa, the Kuralts settled into the apartment on Middagh Street in Brooklyn.

Kuralt's job had him sifting through reams of wire copy from the Associated Press, United Press and Reuters, as well as the night's cables from CBS News' foreign bureaus. He condensed the best of it all into a five-minute radio newscast for the announcer to read on the air at 2 a.m.

Then Kuralt did it all over again for the hourly broadcasts until 6 a.m.

His writing talent was quickly recognized. After a week of substituting for a vacationing writer on Murrow's nightly broadcast, Kuralt was promoted from radio to television, where he joined the writing team for the network's big news program, "CBS Evening News with Douglas Edwards."

Not only was it a day job, but the experience gave Kuralt a tremendous education about how to meld words and pictures. Fellow staff writer Alice Weel was his teacher. "Don't ever let your words fight the pictures," she told him. "Pictures are so strong that, in a fight, they always win."

It was a lesson he never forgot. Nor did he forget Weel. In a 1997 letter to "Sunday Morning" colleague Alison Owings, Kuralt wrote:

The senior writer in 1957 was Alice Weel, who ate pencils. I don't mean merely chewed them, but sometimes actually consumed them. Her lips at the end of the day were shaded Eberhard #2. She did not shrink even from the erasers and the little bands of metal that held the erasers on. It must

have been a tense job, even then. But Alice was not
arrogant, merely flaky, and she was talented. She taught me
how to write to film. I cannot imagine where she learned,
but everything she told me was right, and I still believe it
all, and try to share it with writers starting out.

One of those Kuralt shared Weel's wisdom with was Dan Rather. Over a beer, he advised the future heir to the CBS News throne to "let the film talk to you. Listen to the pictures, then write to them as you would write to music." Rather knew and appreciated what he was being told. After Kuralt's death, he described Kuralt's television essays as "miniature movies ... they had breadth, depth and sweep to engage the eye, ear and mind."

From his first desk on the set of the "Evening News," young Kuralt looked across a wide hall into the network's newsroom. The reporters in that hub came from newspaper jobs, as had Kuralt, and over time he grew to envy them and the urgency of their work.

After a little more than a year of writing for the "Evening News," he was looking for a way to move back to reporting, and it came in the shape of a job called reporter-contact. The person in charge of this job assigned free-lance cameramen to cover local news, but occasionally the reporter-contact went out himself. Although he was forced to take a cut in pay and return to working the graveyard shift, the report-contact became Kuralt's ticket to the front of the camera.

His first assignment was covering Chinese New Year. When a cherry bomb exploded at his feet, he uttered his first words on CBS News, "Wow, that one nearly got me, Al."

Despite the awkward start, before long he began to win praise for his news coverage. In 1959, CBS made him its youngest-ever news correspondent. He was 24.

The position opened a new world to Kuralt, one that he clearly enjoyed to the hilt. He was there for the opening of the St. Lawrence Seaway in 1959 and boasted to his old college pal Ed Yoder Jr. that he was the first reporter through the first lock of the seaway. "I was in the bow of the boat," Kuralt quipped.

In 1960, CBS launched "Eyewitness to History" and tapped Walter Cronkite to anchor the Friday night news program. But Cronkite had to bow out. It was a year of historic news events, including the Kennedy-Nixon presidential race, and he had no time. So CBS News President Sig Mickelson decided to take a chance on Kuralt.

"Eyewitness to History" catapulted Kuralt into what he called "the best job I've ever had." The job paid $30,000 a year and propelled him to celebrity status. In *Variety* magazine, he was heralded as "a comer. Young, good-looking, full of poise and command, deep-voiced and yet relaxed and not over-dramatic, he imparts a sense of authority and reliability to his task."

"This is it, something I've always wanted to do," he told the *Raleigh News & Observer* in 1960. "I write as well as report, and I have something to say about what goes into the program."

That same year *Newsweek* speculated that this quickly rising star was "heir-apparent to the Ed Murrow throne." Kuralt ridiculed such notions. "It's a little like going to work for *The New York Times* and imagining that you're going to take over Jim Reston's job."

"Eyewitness to History" was built around the big news story of the week, with the anchor trekking wherever in the world the news was happening. The travel thrilled Kuralt. "I bought a trench coat and waited for the phone to ring," he wrote in *A Life on the Road*.

In 1960, CBS named Kuralt the roving anchor for "Eyewitness to History," which required him to buy a trench coat and travel to the far-flung corners of the globe.

He traveled to the Congo, where he reported on that country's bloody struggle for independence. He went to Cuba in the days when Castro was still a guerrilla in the Sierra Maestra. He traveled to New Orleans, where a mob of screaming white parents tried to prevent a 6-year-old black girl from entering a public school.

With Kuralt as the roving anchor, "Eyewitness" won a basic audience share of 25, meaning that one in every four TV sets turned on Friday at 10:30 p.m. was tuned to the show.

As nourishing as this success was for Kuralt's ego and ambitions, the demands were having a devastating effect on his marriage and family life. He wrote in *A Life on the Road* that he became drunk with travel and "dizzy with the import of it all." After five years of marriage to Sory, it was all over. She returned to North Carolina with Lisa and a second daughter, Susan.

Soon, his professional life began to suffer. After Kuralt's meteoric rise to anchor "Eyewitness," Jim Aubrey, head of CBS television, launched an anti-Kuralt campaign, complaining the anchor was "low-key, slow, not what you want." There was no love lost between them. In *A Life on the Road*, Kuralt said those who worked for Aubrey called him the "Smiling Cobra." Mickelson and "Eyewitness" Producer Les Midgley tried to fight back, but to no avail. In 1961, Cronkite was installed as anchor. After serving briefly as a field reporter for "Eyewitness," Kuralt was shipped out of the country.

"Charlie was sent to South America where he was a correspondent, the only correspondent that the network had on the whole continent," Midgley said. "It was a bad thing to do to him after he had worked so well and so hard."

Brazil was not at all where Kuralt had thought his career was going, and he was lonely there. Two years after divorcing Sory, Kuralt married again. The bride was Suzanna "Petie"

Producer of "Eyewitness to History," Les Midgley was happy with Kuralt as anchor. But the network bosses felt the 26-year-old was too "low-key." When Walter Cronkite became the show's new anchor, Kuralt was shipped off to South America. Recently divorced and all alone, he was the only CBS correspondent on the whole continent.

Baird, secretary to Douglas Edwards. The wedding was a one-minute ceremony at New York's City Hall on June 1, 1962. Kuralt and Baird thought they were sneaking away to quietly marry. But on their wedding day, several news organizations, including CBS, were at City Hall to do a story on June brides. The newlyweds bumped right into the CBS News crew.

Following their marriage, the Kuralts traveled to Brazil. Then in 1963, CBS moved them back to the United States, to Los Angeles, where Kuralt marked time as chief West Coast correspondent. As he had done at the *Charlotte News*, Kuralt discovered he was not cut out for hard news. Several times, he was scooped by rival reporters, and not quite a year into the job, CBS recalled him to New York. "Having decided that I was a washout as a reporter of breaking stories," Kuralt wrote in *A Life on the Road*, "my bosses assigned me to work on documentaries."

He enjoyed documentaries, and early on floated the idea of the "On the Road" series to Fred Friendly. The CBS News president called it a waste of time.

Kuralt was traveling a great deal. And when he was home from his far-flung assignments, he did his best to stay away from CBS headquarters. He wanted nothing to do with the meetings and demands of the office. He liked to drive the back roads in his Jaguar, "out there where the office can't get hold of me," as he put it in a 1965 interview with the *Chapel Hill Weekly*.

The network sent him on assignments that taxed both his temperament and his physique. While puffing on a Pall Mall cigarette, he told the *Chapel Hill Weekly* reporter: "It's a feverish pace, and sometimes at the end of the day, I think about my health. But you know, I think what keeps people going is their fascination by their work. Guys work 50 years, retire, then have a heart attack. There's something almost meta-

As the news cranked on, Kuralt kept up a cheerful pace, and the broadcasts delighted viewers. Time *magazine, in its January 19, 1968, issue, saw "On the Road" the way most of America did—as a "two-minute cease-fire" sandwiched between the daily barrage of riots, wars and demonstrations on the nightly news. Barely two years old, the series claimed an Emmy and a Peabody Award in 1969. The three-month experiment was on the way to becoming a 13-year, 650-segment phenomenon.*

physical about staying keen. If you ever got bored, I'm sure it would be injurious to your health. In a way the healthiest thing you can do is kind of stay interested. I really confess to not being bored."

He lit another cigarette.

"Yes, I confess to being a chain smoker," he added. "Why should I stop? I couldn't live 10 waking minutes without a cigarette in my hand."

In 1966, Kuralt wrote to CBS colleague Hughes Rudd that he was tired of work of all kinds, having put in crushing long hours on eight or nine shows. "I sit here at the desk vicariously playing golf and undressing passing secretaries and otherwise mentally disporting." He told Rudd he was concerned about his weight and was enduring a diet of celery, Tab and steak and "becoming thinner."

In the summer of 1967, Kuralt tried again to sell CBS on his idea of "On the Road." This time his pitch fell on friendlier ears, those of Dick Salant, the new president of CBS News.

Salant gave Kuralt the green light for a three-month, low-budget project. Kuralt's brief agenda: to find out if the mood of American life really was as unsettled as it appeared on television. To discover that, he would travel to the unheralded small towns of the country.

The series originally was to be named "Travels with Charley," after the John Steinbeck book. But Kuralt said he never had been "particularly fond" of the book and "besides, Charley was a dog." Steinbeck's estate reportedly denied permission to use the title anyway, so "On the Road" it became.

In October of 1967, Kuralt and cameraman Jim Wilson set out with a sound and light crew in an old Dodge Travco rented from the National Geographic Society. They headed to New England, where they filed their first show, a two-minute report from a leaf-strewn road in Vermont. Kuralt began the broadcast with: "It is death that causes this blinding show of color. But it is a fierce and flaming death." The segment was a huge hit back at CBS.

While rolling through Ohio a month later, Kuralt noticed that every town except Harrisburg was plastered with campaign posters. The town, population 360, had "managed to escape all the unseemly excitement of Election Day by the simple expedient that nobody was running for anything." The town treasurer "just never got around to putting her name on the ballot."

Kuralt was back to doing what he loved best, and he became a master at extracting the story he wanted. He had a way of making his subjects feel comfortable, even with a camera in their faces, according to Jane Tolbert, a masters student from the University of Florida who traveled with the "On the Road" crew in 1974.

Kuralt gave Tolbert a behind-the-scenes look into how he loosened up his interview subjects: "I might just say to the guy, 'What in the hell are you doing way out here in the piney woods with a library?' The guy sees I'm at ease. Pretty soon he thinks, 'Well, if this guy can be kinda fat and not have his hair combed and talk like that, maybe I can just be myself, too.'"

By 1980, "On the Road" had collected 12 Emmys and worn out six campers. Kuralt was also beginning to wear out. In the spring of 1980, he was arrested and pleaded *nolo contendere* to drunk driving on the West Coast. A year earlier, he started anchoring "Sunday Morning," a leisurely 90-minute show created around his poetic storytelling and curiosity. But anchoring meant he had to return to New York every weekend, and soon the romance of the road wore thin.

In the fall of 1980, he parked the van for good, became a full-time resident of Greenwich Village and took on the additional position of anchor of CBS's weekday "Morning" show. He thought the routine would be good for his life.

But barely a year into being settled, he confessed the job bored him. "You can't be a reporter anymore once you've started doing this, and I have certain little wistful regrets about that," he told the *Washington Journalism Review* in 1981.

The "Morning" show was consuming. Kuralt went to bed at 6 p.m., arose around midnight, brewed a cup of coffee and read some history, which he had maintained a passion for since his days at UNC. He took a taxi to the office at 3 a.m.— refusing the network's limousine service—and started writing and rewriting the news. In the *WJR* interview, Kuralt said, "I find I'm always exhausted and there's a constant subconscious tension running through me now."

But the more viewers saw of Kuralt, the more they wanted. When he substituted for Walter Cronkite on "CBS Evening News" for several weeks, ratings soared and mail poured in. It was enough to raise speculation that the network had made the wrong choice in choosing Dan Rather to succeed Cronkite in 1981.

Would Kuralt have taken that job if it had been offered? Many close to him say no. It is difficult to say whether Kuralt was serious when he told the *Tar Heel* magazine in 1982 that he would have considered the slot because "after all, it's better hours."

In 1981, Kuralt's salary grew from $160,000 to $200,000 a year. Meanwhile, Rather was making a reported $8 million in salary and benefits over five years, and NBC's Tom Brokaw was raking in a reported $15 million over seven years.

Kuralt refused to have an agent negotiate his contract with CBS. "Every five years, I'd go in, they'd make an offer, and I'd say OK," Kuralt told North Carolina's *The State* magazine in 1996. "It would last about 10 minutes."

In a December 1, 1978, letter to old friend Katherine Henson, Kuralt wrote: "Thanks for your birthday card ... it was the only birthday card I got, except one from the liquor store. Of news, there is but little ... just finished reading proof on a book—not much of a book, a collection of radio pieces to come out in the spring, but it was fun debating 'any more.' I said two words, Harcourt Brace Jovanovich said one. To hell with them. I am going through and changing every 'any more' to 'any longer,' a loss. Also, starting Jan. 28, I am going to park the bus on weekends to do a Sunday morning hour and a half broadcast called: 'Sunday Morning!' It may be good. I haven't much hope that whatever N.C. CBS station you see will clear away enough Tulsa evangelists to actually carry the thing ... "

Charlotte friend Jim Babb thought CBS was underpaying Kuralt. Babb once offered to negotiate on his old friend's behalf. "I told him, 'Charles, it's time for you to get what you deserve from CBS. Get yourself an agent. Let me do it. I'll do it for nothing. You deserve a big payoff here. You've been loyal. You are the only one in the whole television journalism business who isn't getting what he deserves,'" Babb said. "Two days later, he goes in and signs the contract, doesn't even ask CBS to up the ante."

Kuralt also turned down commercial opportunities, Babb said. "I know he turned down a $3 million deal to do a commercial for a pharmaceutical company two years before his death," Babb said. "Here was a chance for him to get a big payoff late in his career, and he says no, because he didn't want to be commercialized."

In 1992, CBS sent Kuralt to Albertville, France, where he did "On the Road" type pieces for the Winter Olympics. Kuralt would end each day's work in a pizzeria with producer Peter Schweitzer. "He spoke no French, and the owners spoke no English," Schweitzer said in an interview later on. "But they loved him, and he loved them. They called him, 'Doublescotch.'"

Two years later (because of a decision to switch to a two-year cycle between Summer and Winter Olympics), at the 17th Olympic Winter Games in Lillehammer, Kuralt decided to call it a day. He returned to New York, tendered his resignation, and on April 3, 1994, sat at the "Sunday Morning" easel for the final time. He had amassed 13 Emmys and three Peabodys for his work in television.

When it was proposed that Kuralt go "On the Road" and file features for the "Evening News," Walter Cronkite objected. But with the first installment, the respected anchorman was sold.

The Eagle
Has Landed

—

WALTER CRONKITE
CBS Colleague

W ALTER CRONKITE ADMITS HE SUFFERED a little envy when Charles Kuralt came to CBS in 1957. Admiring editors passed Kuralt's copy around the newsroom, and Cronkite read it with the same wonder as the rest. "Here was a guy born the very year I got my first full-time newspaper job and already he wrote a lot better than I did," Cronkite said.

Even so, Cronkite confesses he had grave reservations about allowing a new series called "On the Road" to fill air space on his "Evening News."

"I was opposed to doing any regular features that we promised would be on the air, because I felt the broadcast had to follow the principle of news first, features second," Cronkite said. "And if we had a feature that we just had to get into the show each week or so, it would be restrictive of us who were trying to do the news."

But Kuralt's first installment from Vermont instantly won

him over. "I saw that it was so extraordinary that it would add something to the 'Evening News' that no other broadcast had," he said.

Cronkite watched as Kuralt absorbed accolade after accolade over the years, and through it all Kuralt remained unfazed. "He accepted the many, many awards that would be bestowed upon him, and he sat through untold numbers of speeches of praise," Cronkite said. "But none of that was able to pierce his cloak of humility."

A year before Kuralt's death, Cronkite himself presented his colleague with an award—for distinguished journalism. In accepting, Kuralt had great fun telling a story about CBS's special coverage of the Bicentennial celebration in 1976.

Cronkite anchored that broadcast in the studio. Kuralt was aboard the Coast Guard ship *Eagle* in a parade of great sailing ships. "The band was playing aboard the *Eagle*, bands were playing on shore, fireboats were spraying great red, white and blue plumes of water into the air, crowds were cheering," Kuralt recalled. "It was the patriotic equivalent of all hell breaking loose."

Back in the control room, cue cards urgently told Cronkite: "Go to Kuralt." "But Walter was involved in a long and tedious history of the discovery of America with a guest to whom he wanted to be polite, the naval historian Samuel Eliot Morison. 'Go to Kuralt,' said the cue card. But Cronkite was genuinely interested in this interview. He asked Morison another impenetrably dull question, and Morison obediently droned on.

"I said, 'The *Eagle* passing the Battery was a great, historic moment,' and it was. It was a moment. It passed. The band stopped playing. The guns stopped firing. The fireboats ran out of red, white and blue water. The crowds were left behind. We entered the Hudson River on a tide of silence. There was nothing to see and nothing to hear and nothing for me to say.

"In the midst of my disappointment, in my headset I heard Walter say, 'Fascinating, Admiral Morison. Thank you for being with us for this historic morning, and now let's go to Charles Kuralt aboard the *Eagle*.'"

O N THE DAY KURALT DIED, Cronkite, the man who was affectionately nicknamed "Old Iron Pants" for his unflappability under pressure, broke down in tears.

THE FOREST FOR THE TREES

One Friday, I was laboring and belaboring a lead-in to a piece for "Sunday Morning" about a program that helped young drug addicts get clean. I was gumming over the phrase about "not seeing the forest for the trees" and got stuck in the forest. Finally, because of the press of time or a sense of futility, I left it, unhappily and flummoxed.

Charles habitually came to work Saturday morning. Thus he had my awkward forest and trees lead-in. When I reported to work Sunday about 6:30 a.m., I read the then-retyped and print-ed script, secretly looking to see what of mine he had used or tossed. There was one week when he changed nothing, and I felt I'd won the Pulitzer. But he changed forest and trees. Inspired, understated, he wrote that with all the drug programs and all the addicts—words to this effect—sometimes one cannot see the **trees** *for the* **forest**. *That's it, I thought, shaking my head. He got it.*

—Alison Owings, writer, CBS "Sunday Morning"

Kuralt once told me that he did not write a single word until he had a picture in his mind. That was his genius. He juxtaposed words over pictures and pictures over words.

—Bernie Birnbaum

Picture Perfect

BERNIE BIRNBAUM
CBS Colleague

I N 1962, WHEN AMERICANS WERE FIRST barred from entering
Cuba, Kuralt scored a coup, wangling his way onto the
Caribbean island. As chief of CBS's Latin American
bureau, he had managed to secure a special visa for himself
through the consular offices in Rio de Janeiro. The only snag
was that he had to go solo, without camera crew or support
staff.

As a coup, it very nearly failed. In Havana, a Foreign
Ministry bureaucrat accused Kuralt of using a ruse to obtain
the visa and ordered him out of the country on the next possible flight. Luckily for Kuralt, all seats were booked for three
weeks.

In the meantime, he set about exploring the capital with
a hand-held Bell & Howell 16-millimeter camera and 50 rolls
of black-and-white film. He shot footage of a May Day workers' and peasants' parade. He visited the poor parts of Havana,
filming food stores and their virtually empty shelves.

Government officials tried to steer him toward the things they wanted the world to see, but Kuralt sought out the real Cuba.

At the airport the day he left, a guard confiscated every roll of film. Kuralt put up a big argument, but it was just for show. He had already arranged for the real film to be shipped by special diplomatic pouch to Mexico City and then to CBS headquarters in New York.

The footage contained the first American views of Cuba in more than a year. Halfway through screening at CBS, Les Midgley turned to Bernie Birnbaum and said, "Bernie, why can't our New York cameramen shoot this well?"

Kuralt shot so well because he fully understood the relationship between pictures and words, Birnbaum said years later. In the cutting room, Kuralt meticulously orchestrated his script with the film, down to telling a technician, "I want this word to hit over this particular frame."

But if pictures gave life to Kuralt's words, his words also gave life to the pictures. In 1964, CBS called on Kuralt's talents for an episode titled "Christmas in Appalachia."

"This is a road, if you can call it that, that leads to the Pert Creek School in Letcher County, Kentucky," Kuralt began. "There are tens of thousands of roads like this, winding back along the creeks and hollows of 11 states. And beside these roads, the shacks and tarpaper and pine, which are the home of a million permanently poor."

Scenes of poverty mixed with Kuralt's poignant message moved the hearts of viewers. The CBS switchboard lit up. Unsolicited, viewers donated $70,000, which the network gave to the Red Cross. One viewer chartered a plane to carry food and Christmas presents to Appalachia. "That was the impact his words had," Birnbaum said. "And this was before the War on Poverty."

AMERICAN MADE

I was struck by the fact that Charlie died on the fourth of July, because he was a patriot in the truest sense of the word. He believed in the idea and in the ideals of America—as a nation of immigrants and individualists. Before he embarked "On the Road," to report the part of the American story he loved the most, we spent part of the 1960s together. During the turmoil of the civil rights and anti-Vietnam war movements and the growth of an American counter-culture, we found much to agree on—and much to argue about. For one thing, he insisted that baseball, not football, was the game that truly reflected America.

Those were wrenching days, producing a clash of values and of visions, and a debate over the meaning of patriotism. But on this issue, Charlie was unshakable. He reacted in kind to those who would condemn the demonstrators and flower children and to those, like myself, who found in the flag decals and slogans attached to numerous rigs and pickups evidence of an intolerant backwater. For Charlie, the right to wave the flag was not a matter of philosophy, or class, or of politics. Old Glory was a symbol of our freedoms, and belonged to all Americans.

—Irv Drasnin, former CBS News producer

Kuralt maintained that he floated the concept of "On the Road" to CBS News presidents Fred Friendly and Dick Salant, but a few days before our interview, Andy Rooney ran across a memo he had written years ago suggesting the idea of touring the country and doing little stories for the "Evening News." He thought Harry Reasoner should be the one to do it. "Ultimately Harry decided that he didn't want to be away from home that much," Rooney said, "so they gave it to Charles."

Consummate Craftsman

ANDY ROONEY
CBS Colleague

A NDY ROONEY AND CHARLES KURALT covered nearly a dozen political conventions together, working shoulder to shoulder at times, each with his own camera crew. "I was always distraught when I watched what I had done and what Charlie had done," Rooney said. "I did what I thought were some good pieces, but his were always better."

To Rooney, celebrated in his own right for his Emmy-winning closing segments for "60 Minutes," Kuralt did everything better than anybody else in television. And the remarkable thing was that "the rest of us never resented him for doing better. It was because Kuralt was without an edge himself. He genuinely enjoyed it when other people did things well."

Kuralt was so good at what he did that "60 Minutes" twice tried to steal him away, and each time Kuralt refused. At an awards dinner honoring "60 Minutes" Executive Producer Don Hewitt, Kuralt explained why. It went back, he said, to

Charles Kuralt, at age 26, interviews North Carolina governor Luther Hodges at the 1960 Democratic National Convention in Los Angeles. Kuralt and CBS colleague Andy Rooney covered nearly a dozen national elections together, providing CBS with vignettes of people and features about the election. "I remember sitting back and thinking, My gosh, he's better than I am," Rooney said. "I don't do that with many people."

the early days when he was writing copy for the Douglas Edwards news show and Hewitt was an associate director. Each night Kuralt would strive to craft at least one paragraph to perfection, and consistently, when the script ran long, Hewitt would cross it out. "I've known for a long while that Don Hewitt knows good writing when he sees it," Kuralt told the awards dinner audience, "and he doesn't want any part of it."

Rooney puts Kuralt in the same league as Ralph Waldo Emerson, Henry David Thoreau, even Mark Twain, but doubts his friend will join these exalted writers in the history books. "The things people do in television go up in smoke, and even if it's saved on tape, it isn't as if it was in a library and could be read and reread by schoolchildren as Mark Twain and so many of the great writers have been," he said. "Even as good as Charles was, he's not going to be remembered for his writing on television. I just don't think his memory is going to last, and it's sad."

On the day the call came saying Kuralt had died, Rooney wept. He was home on vacation, tinkering in his woodworking shop. His tears left rust spots on his big steel saw table. But while Rooney grieved, he was also angry. "He made us all love him and then he left us without himself," Rooney said, referring to Kuralt's constant roaming. "He often did that."

But Kuralt had to keep moving. "That's why he left CBS," Rooney said. "No matter where he was, he wanted to go some place else. He loved North Carolina, but I've been in North Carolina with him, and whenever he was there, he wanted to leave."

In the end, Kuralt did choose North Carolina as his final resting place. A tombstone marks the spot at the Old Chapel Hill Cemetery. "But I know Charles," Rooney said. "And I know he won't be content there either."

When Harry Reasoner left for ABC, "60 Minutes" Producer Don Hewitt asked Philip Scheffler, above, to recruit Kuralt. "We had dinner one night, and I said [to Kuralt], 'You know, why don't you go to work for '60 Minutes?' That's a really great opportunity.' He said, '... I just couldn't abide that kind of pressure.' I think he was wise not to accept."

Unchanging

PHILIP SCHEFFLER
Executive Editor "60 Minutes"

W HEN KURALT CAME TO CBS IN 1957, he quickly
struck up a friendship with Philip Scheffler, who
was already a veteran of five years at the fledgling
network. They became good friends both on and off the job,
working and traveling together for "Eyewitness to History"
and even sharing vacations. Eventually, the Schefflers and the
Kuralts bought a vacation home together in Essex,
Connecticut. They went abroad together, and several times
chartered sailboats in the Virgin Islands, the Chesapeake and
New England.

They were friends, but nothing alike. Scheffler was a
native New Yorker; Kuralt, a country boy from North
Carolina. When "Eyewitness" sent them on one of their first
trips together, to Guatemala, it was clear which was which as
soon as the taxi deposited them at their hotel. Scheffler
stepped out and proceeded straight to the lobby, while Kuralt
stayed behind with the driver to help unload the bags. In later

years, Kuralt joked that one of the reasons he resented working with producers was that he always had to carry the bags.

Kuralt was teasing, but the incident underscored his character. Rather than summon someone's help, he preferred to do what needed to be done. He rarely complained publicly or to people he worked with. "If something bothered him," Scheffler said, "he would just do something to correct it."

It was that way when Kuralt quit CBS. He disliked the way the network was treating his show, "Sunday Morning," so he walked in and resigned. "Instead of going to the management and saying, 'I demand that you do this,' or 'I'm going to leave if you don't do this,' and on and on and on like that, he just left," Scheffler said. "That was so typical, so exactly typical of the kind of person he was."

The same trait appeared in his private life. After sharing the vacation house for four years, he asked Scheffler to buy him out. Kuralt said he was on the road so much that he preferred not to pay half the mortgage and upkeep when he used the house so little. "But that wasn't the real reason," Scheffler said. "I think he was still bothered that my wife had slipped a place mat under his coffee cup one morning. He wouldn't complain, but he had no intention of living that way. So we gained half a house, and after a while he bought the house next door where, presumably, he could put his cup down any damn place he chose."

While Kuralt was no complainer, he never let others tell him what to do. When Scheffler suggested he give up cigarettes and stop eating so much, he got angry. "He'd say, 'I'm healthier than you are. I could beat you at a 100-yard dash right now. Let's go. Come on. We'll go out and race down the road.' And he would mean it," Scheffler said.

(After heart surgery in 1995, Kuralt told a *TV Guide* reporter that he had no intention to stop smoking. "Smoking brings great pleasure to me," he said. "I am going to be more attentive to my health, but I don't want to overdo it. There's a self-centeredness in American life that is quite unattractive. I don't want to concentrate on living to be 100, spending an hour a day on the treadmill and another hour eating a salt-free dinner. It's outside my philosophy.")

Kuralt was "physically unprepossessing," Scheffler said, and when on the road, he could often go unrecognized. In his "On the Road" series, the camera was seldom turned on him.

In the 40 years of their friendship, Scheffler saw very little change in Charles Kuralt—in the way he looked at the world or in his broadcasting style. In a tribute to Kuralt in early 1999, New York's Museum of Broadcasting played a reel of Kuralt's early broadcasts, including Christmas in Appalachia. "If you closed your eyes, you were listening to Edward Murrow," Scheffler said. "The pauses and even the timbre of his voice was exactly like Murrow's."

Kuralt, of course, developed his own style over the years. But looking back over four decades, Scheffler said the Kuralt he knew stayed true to his course. "I would say that he changed less than anybody I know."

What makes a good story? That's a hard question to answer. The yardstick I always used was just if something interested me or amused me, if I liked the guy and was interested in the story myself, I just assumed other people would be too. You're always looking—for what we used to call in the "On the Road" bus—you're looking for a talker, somebody who enjoys using the language, somebody who is not too reticent about whatever it is he's doing. And, of course, the woods are just full of people like that, people who are wonderful talkers. Once you get into the American South it's hard to get out if you're looking for characters.

—Charles Kuralt in 1994
interview with Ralph Grizzle

Waiting for Roger

IZZY BLECKMAN
CBS Colleague

L OOKING FOR STORIES ON THE BACK ROADS of Ohio, Kuralt and the "On the Road" crew passed a farmhouse with a homemade yellow banner stretched between two oaks in the front yard. The banner read, "Welcome Home, Roger!" Thinking nothing of it, the crew rolled on. But a few miles down the road, Kuralt turned to the driver of the bus, cameraman Izzy Bleckman. "You know," he said. "We ought to go back there and find out who Roger is."

Roger, they learned, was a soldier coming home from the war in Vietnam. His friends and family had strung up the yellow banner and gathered in the front yard to give him a soldier's welcome. Roger's mother baked a cake. Roger's wife awaited her husband nursing a baby he had never seen.

Kuralt talked with the folks gathered, while Bleckman shot scenes of people peering down the road for Roger's imminent arrival. Bleckman shot for about an hour, panning through the house, where photographs of Roger adorned the

Mornings I'd go out early, start up the generator, get some coffee going and work on my cameras. Finally, Charles would come out after he had had some breakfast. He'd have a cup of coffee, light a cigarette, bring a newspaper along, all the time thinking about how he was going to write the story we had just shot. And he'd keep putting it off, one cigarette, two cigarettes. He would read the newspaper, walk around, sit down, get up, fix his coffee, put a little cream in it, not enough cream, put some more cream in it, look out the window. It was as though sitting down and writing was maybe a little painful. After about an hour of this, he'd take the typewriter out, put some paper in it, scroll it up and write some little notes on it. Then he'd just pound the story right out.

—Izzy Bleckman

walls. The crew was just settling in when Kuralt announced it was time to go. Their departure seemed premature to Bleckman, who said, "Yeah, but we ..."

"We don't need to see Roger," Kuralt interrupted. "It's better if we don't."

To Bleckman's astonishment, Kuralt was serious. They got back on the bus and drove away, and Kuralt started typing his story. The segment aired the next night on the "Evening News," and the CBS switchboard was swamped. To the viewers, the unseen Roger represented all of the GIs coming home to their families from Southeast Asia.

"He was right," Bleckman said. "He was always right about things like that. Today we'd wait for Roger until the cows came home, and we'd shoot the hell out of it. We'd interview him for three hours. And the wonder of who Roger was and all the rest of it, I mean, the whole story would just come to collapse."

While Kuralt knew when to leave, he began not to want to. "We'd make contact with these folks, and they were so wonderful," Bleckman said. "We got very close to them, but then the time would come when we would have to get on the bus and go on down the road. And it would just take forever to say goodbye, because we were reluctant to leave."

Back on the road, they settled quietly back into their routines. Sound man Larry Gianneschi would take the backseat, where he worked on crossword puzzles. Charlie Quinlan, the electrician, would take the front passenger seat. Kuralt sat at the dinette, which held his typewriter.

"He would just light a cigarette and look out the window," Bleckman said. "And it would be awhile before we all started talking about anything, because we were still kind of back there. We were still in the place we had just left."

The "On the Road" crew worked 10 days to two weeks at

a time, depending on the nature and location of the stories. "Charles always said the best schedule was to drive the least amount the next day, and that way we always had a destination where we'd do another story with the prospect of finding one on the way," Bleckman said.

While traveling together strengthened the bond between Kuralt and Bleckman, it took its toll on Bleckman's marriage. In 1988, his wife of 20 years tired of waiting for him to come home and asked for a divorce. The settlement was going to be costly; he faced losing the Chicago house he built mostly with his own hands. When he shared his fears with Kuralt on the phone, his friend suggested they meet for dinner. "You know, I'm on my way to Los Angeles," Kuralt said. "Why don't you meet me at the airport? I'll stop off and overnight at O'Hare. Come out and have dinner with me."

Over dinner, Kuralt came right to the point. "Would $50,000 help you keep your house?" Bleckman said it would, but he did not want to take Kuralt's money. Kuralt insisted. "We don't need to talk about this again," he said. "Just pay me back when you can." And with that, Kuralt wrote him a check for $50,000. It took Bleckman five years, but he did repay his old buddy.

When Kuralt died on July 4, 1997, "it just dusted me away," Bleckman said. They had planned to get together over the weekend. Kuralt told Bleckman from the hospital: 'I'm feeling better. They've finally figured it out. I'm going to be out of here on the weekend. You can come up to Essex when I'm out.'"

Bleckman was in Buffalo, checking his voice mail messages. One was from Kuralt's secretary. "She was crying, and she didn't even get to the point of why she was crying," Bleckman said. "And then she said, 'Charles is gone.'"

LISTENING

In the first couple of months of working together, Bleckman filmed Kuralt conducting an interview at the Iowa state fair. After several minutes, Kuralt motioned for Bleckman to stop filming. Bleckman shut off the camera and walked away. Kuralt stayed and talked. "When it was all over, Charles walked over to me and put his arm around my shoulder," Bleckman said. "He told me that I wasn't listening. And he wasn't upset, but he was concerned, concerned that this new guy wasn't going to work out. He said that it was important to listen to what the people had to say, because that was everything. I never forgot that. Now when I film an interview, I hear what's going to be used."

It was hard for Kuralt and Izzy Bleckman to get over the "perfectly understandable idea" that they had to have a destination in mind. "We always had an idea of a story we were headed toward, but it finally got through to us that we might run into something more interesting along the way," Kuralt said. "After awhile we carefully never made precise appointments. We'd call and say, 'Are you going to be home for the next week or two?' Because we knew that we wouldn't be able to get there Tuesday at 10 o'clock in the morning, very likely."

On The Road

JANE T. TOLBERT
Graduate Student

I N THE WEEKS BEFORE CHRISTMAS 1974, Jane Tolbert, a master's student at the University of Florida, traveled with Kuralt and the "On the Road" crew for her thesis in Journalism and Communications. Today, Tolbert teaches at Florida Tech in Melbourne, where she still makes use of her "On the Road" experience. "When a few students complain they can't write a profile, because the interviewee was 'too boring' or 'too trite,' I remind them of Kuralt's words, 'Everyone has a story to tell,'" Tolbert said. Following is Tolbert's account of her on-the-road experience with Charles Kuralt.

More than 25 years ago, I set off on a journey with the "On the Road" crew as part of a study on Charles Kuralt's writing and production techniques. I met up with Kuralt, Izzy Bleckman, Larry Gianneschi and Charlie Quinlan in Reno. Together in that white motor home with the CBS logo, we headed across Donner Pass. Our destination was Santa Cruz, where the crew planned to do a story on Tom Scribner, a musical saw player of the Lost Sound Band.

For me, like for many other journalists, Kuralt was a hero. He exhibited a unique blend of skills—an eloquent style and a boundless curiosity coupled with a broad knowledge of literature and history. Most important, he had a sincere interest in people and wanted to show what he described as "individualism in this age of plastics and conformity." Through his series, he introduced viewers to diverse vocations—a horse trader, a backwoods Thoreau, a miller— insisting that these individuals were not insignificant, only little known. Just as a successful artist captures a scene with a few brush strokes, Kuralt selected words and quotes to convey the distinctive features of a person's life and compress it into a few minutes of air time.

Kuralt maintained he had no philosophy behind the series. But in his travels on interstates and back roads, he captured the individualism of America. He found "value" in reminding viewers of the importance of the continuity of daily activities in the face of crime and violence, a perspective that many of us long for today.

My travels "On the Road" with the crew for two weeks showed me another side of Kuralt—the private Kuralt. He was unselfish. At the end of the day he patiently answered my questions and talked about his work. He told me about the inception of the series when he and a cameraman were on an airplane and noticed the tiny specks of light below, each light representing a story to tell. Kuralt was modest in sharing his knowledge of the trade, and he took little credit for the success of the series. Instead, he talked about his reliance on the expertise of Izzy, Larry and Charlie.

The crew spent much of each day in a 23-foot motor

home yet maintained a spirit of collegiality. We made stops—at a pub in San Francisco for Irish coffee, one of the crew's favorite watering holes; a Chinese restaurant in Santa Cruz, where we dined on cracked rice soup; and Point Lobos, where we stopped to admire the scenery. All the time, Kuralt seemed pleasantly surprised when people on the street recognized him (particularly if they asked if he had lost weight.) Between our stops and trips to the airport to drop off a story for editing in New York, the crew began filming for other stories—one about unusual license plates and another about laundry blowing in the wind.

The Kuralt series was, of course, the antithesis of a studio production. This was no place for a prima donna. The working relationship was one of mutual respect. The small crew worked professionally and in perfect choreography. Unlike many of today's carefully scripted productions, nothing was rehearsed for "On the Road." Kuralt even refused to approach a story with a well-defined idea of the end product or to discuss interview questions until the film began rolling. That way he preserved the spontaneity of the response. He stayed with the story until he could visualize the opening and closing shots and the main body of the story. He had a unique ability to meld script and film.

Now, 25 years later, I continue a journey of a different sort. Kuralt continues to be a mentor to my class of communication students. The stories of his that I share, which appear to be effortlessly written, reveal a high level of craftsmanship—word choice, the selection of quotations, and respect for his subjects. Kuralt asked captive questions and knew when to step aside to let the subject tell the story. For many of us these skills are gained only through years of experience. But for Charles Kuralt, it all seemed to come naturally.

BEHIND THE SCENES

In her 1975 thesis, "The Charles Kuralt 'On the Road' Television Series: A Structural and Production Analysis," University of Florida graduate student Jane Tolbert identified Kuralt's series as "an innovative style of reporting not yet duplicated by any of the other major networks."

In the years since her thesis, both the major networks, and the minor ones, have tried to do the type of soft feature that Kuralt elevated into an art form. What made "On the Road" so successful? Kuralt's writing, Tolbert posited in her thesis. While the CBS broadcaster insisted he had no particular style, Tolbert analyzed several scripts and found recurring stylistic themes.

Kuralt, for example, frequently used leads that posed a series of questions. "Do we not all have dreams of glory?" read the opening line for "Bull Fighter." Moreover, Kuralt wrote in a personal style, often using the personal pronouns, "we" or "you," unusual in broadcast journalism when "On the Road" began.

Many "On the Road" segments started with understatement or denial. In a segment called, "Pioneer Grave," Kuralt began, "There's not much to see here. It's just a grave ... "

In the piece "Grist Mill," Kuralt said, "There can't be a 300-year-old grist mill in mid-20th century America ... "

As a former newspaper writer, Kuralt wrote simply, using descriptive adjectives and active verbs as in the following excerpt from "Horse Trader."

> ... Ben K. Green has spent his whole life in corrals and livery stables and wagon yards, cheating, and being cheated, measuring, judging, buying, selling, cursing, currying and talking—horses.

In 1974, Jane Tolbert traveled with Kuralt and the "On the Road" crew for her thesis as a graduate student at the University of Florida.

In addition to his writing style, Kuralt repeated themes that appealed to viewers. One frequently recurring theme was that yankee ingenuity and individualism still exist in this country. Thus, the characters that appeared in "On the Road" often had an intensely consuming interest in something. In the story about Green, the horse-trader, Kuralt wrote: "He is a doctor, philosopher, an author and trader. And what he doctors, philosophizes on, writes about and trades—are horses."

In the backwoods of Arkansas, Kuralt came upon Eddie Lovett, whose passion was books. Lovett, the son of a sharecropper, never received much formal education, but he spent a lifetime accumulating thousands of books, which he read day and night.

In the segment, "Piney Woods Thoreau," Lovett said: "I don't think I've lost anything by gaining knowledge, because I've been told by my father and also other people throughout the world that man's greatest enemy is ignorance. And so, by me pondering in my library, researching, I have declared war upon ignorance, and the more I learn, the more I learn that I need to learn and the more I learn that I don't know—and I aspire to drink very deep from the fountain of knowledge."

By allowing Lovett to tell his story in his words, Kuralt was trying to bring viewers closer to the subject, so that they felt they knew Lovett personally. Kuralt frequently used the technique in other "On the Road" segments. "I always try to get a little bit inside the person," Kuralt said.

For a story he did on Tom Scribner, the musical saw player, Kuralt tried to see what Scribner was doing from his point of view. "And sometimes by looking at it that way, a line will occur to me. 'What he wants is one last tour ... '"

The final script read, "What Tom Scribner would like is one last fling, a vaudeville tour like the one he took before he started his lumberjack career, the one he took in 1915 ... "

No preplanning was done for the "On the Road" pieces. Kuralt believed it was a mistake to show up having decided what the story was going to be. "I remember once we set out to do a story on a bagel bakery—just the kind of amusing and frantic way in which bagels are made," Kuralt said. "But one of the bakers turned out to be a teenager, so what the story was finally was a story about a teenage bagel maker."

Kuralt planned no questions for his interview subjects, either. He asked whatever popped into his head. He figured the questions he asked would be what would have popped into most people's heads to ask. He also refused to talk about the interview or anything relating to the topic before sitting down to do the filming. Instead, he would talk about the weather or anything else. He wanted the interview answers to be unrehearsed.

Kuralt thought it important to have a feeling for the subject. He refused to do stories if he did not like the interviewee or the topic. "If you pretend to care, that shows through," he said.

Where did all the story ideas come from? "On the Road" received about 300 letters each week suggesting people and places to cover. Kuralt found other ideas for stories in the local newspapers. He kept a file by state in the van.

On the October day that the crew struck out for New England in search of their first story, that bank of stories did not exist. After a week passed with no story, Kuralt began to worry if the first idea would ever come. It did—a poetically told piece about fall foliage that aired on October 26, 1967. It was an instant success.

SCRIPT TIPS

This note is written in charity and gratitude for all the good scripts you've been sending us. Just a few things that would make them even better ... Please start paragraphing. I know that'll make the lines a little harder to count, but it will help in the reading immensely ... "So and so and so," Mr. X said, is awkward stuff on radio. "So and so," Mr. X said, "and so and so," is okay, but the best is Mr. X said, "So and so and so," if you know what I mean ... Reading over this note I recognize it is nit-picking and stuffy-sounding. Please forgive all that ... Maybe someday we can actually meet and have a drink!

—Charles Kuralt in a 1966 letter to a scriptwriter

Charles Kuralt, the man who brought slow talking and complete silence to network television—and got away with it.

—Garrison Keillor
Minnesota Public Radio

His Own Man

————

BILL MOYERS
CBS Colleague

I N 1984, CBS CALLED ON BILL MOYERS and Charles Kuralt to co-host a new one-hour prime-time series called "The American Parade." The weekly show was to profile individual Americans—the low and the mighty, the obscure and the well-known.

But Kuralt declined to pair himself with Moyers. "We talked, and he just felt that our styles wouldn't mesh," Moyers said. "He was an admirer of mine and I was of him, but we discussed it at length and he said, 'You know, it's not a matter of personality. It's just that the two kinds of journalism, they don't really make a whole. They will be at odds.'" (*Broadcasting* magazine reported in its March 19, 1984, issue that Moyers was the one who declined.)

Kuralt and Moyers did pose a considerable contrast. Kuralt's forte was personality driven, human-interest pieces, poetically told. Moyers was a hard-news journalist and news analyst, given to expository reporting. Moreover, it was no

Bill Moyers and Charles Kuralt were to co-host a new weekly series called "The American Parade," but Moyers said Kuralt felt their two styles would not mesh.

secret that Kuralt did his best work alone.

Moyers met Kuralt in 1976 when he began the first of two stints at CBS. They were not close buddies, but Moyers said no one knew Kuralt well. "Like many good writers and poets, he had a public persona that was a screen between his private thoughts and the rest of the world," Moyers said. "It wasn't a deceptive screen. It was just that he was a very private person despite being a very public man."

The poet in Kuralt craved what he described as "a little daily consideration to his soul, even at the expense of being a little less well-informed." Sometimes, he said, that meant turning off the radio and TV, throwing aside magazines and newspapers, and spending time contemplating the sun going down.

"He claimed a beat for himself and stayed with it all his life, because it was natural for him and important to cover," Moyers said. "He was not tempted by greater marquees. He never wanted to be a star. Charles knew how to perform, but he didn't want to be a performer."

What Moyers admired most about Kuralt was his faithfulness to his own material. "He had an authenticity that is rare in this business and a capacity to live and work by his own light," Moyers said. "He didn't need instructions or regulations. He was determined to be his own man."

"Sunday Morning" Producer Mary Lou Teel, above, revered Kuralt as a master with words. With the stroke of his pen, he could add luster to a script. He brought the same self-assurance to interviews. After 20 minutes of questioning Lady Bird Johnson, below, about her nationwide beautification project, Kuralt turned to Teel and the cameraman and said "All right, we've got it." If Kuralt said it, they did.

Wordsmith

___

MARY LOU TEEL
Producer, "Sunday Morning"

M ARY LOU TEEL JOINED CBS IN 1979 and worked her way up from desk assistant to writing scripts for the CBS Radio Network in 1983. She and Kuralt crossed paths on a series called "Exploring America."

One of her assignments with Kuralt was to write a two-and-a-half-minute script about the first European visions of the wild new country known as America. She labored for days, writing: "America was 10 feet tall; she carried a spear in her mighty hand. America devoured men; she'd lop off a head for a trophy and keep the rest for dinner. America wore shells and America wore gold. Europe was amazed and sailed home to tell the story." The script talked about how the America the Europeans saw was hardly less amazing than the one they had imagined. She concluded with this sentence: "The old artists tried, on the canvas and on the page, to picture the fabulous reality of the newfound world."

Newsnotes and comment, I'm Charles Kuralt, CBS News.

Snow, after this:

COMMERCIAL:

It snowed in Paris last week. It snowed in Rome ~ ~~too~~ Notre Dame's gargoyles
~wore beards of~
~were bearded with~ snow, ~and~ the Vatican was frosted like a wedding cake.

In Florence, Michelangelo's David kept a frosty watch on the square,
with snow on his curls and ~his furrowed brow~ *shoulders*. ~Actually, it was a replica~
~of David that had to face the cold--the real David had taken shelter indoors~.

There was snow ~,too~ on the gondolas of Venice, snow on the frozen canals.

In Antwerp, the zookeepers let the penquins take a turn around the city---
to check out the wonderful ~white stuff~ *snow.* For the penquins, ~it was just~
like home. In Spain, the snow that usually ~kept~ *keeps* to the ~Pyrenees~ peaks *of the Pyrenee*
drifted down over ~the~ *lowland* cities and towns---muffling the cries of children who
had never seen snow before. There was snow ~even~ on the Cote d'Azur ---
in Marseilles, and Nice. *There was snow nearly everywhere in* ~In fact, snow was general all over~ Europe, ~falling~
~on~ *in* Geneva, and Zurich and Prague. And in this country the snow has been
falling , too. Falling on the New England hills and the church steeples---
falling on the capitol dome. There was snow in the Smokie Mountains, and
in Memphis , Tennessee. It snowed as far south as Houston, Texas ---
and the snow spread a flat blanket across the midwest, drifting up in
the Rockies. Snow fell upon our houses, and our factories and our schools,
fell upon gate posts,and statues,and trees ---reducing everything to ~its~
elemental shapes. Snow swirled in front of headlights, ~spattered~ *mounted on door*
~against window panes~, and quietly covered much of the world. Snow fell in
places last week where it hasn't snowed in years. *before* ~The~ people must have
marvelled to see their world transformed ---made as simple as a snow drift hunched
against a house, and as delicate as a filigree of frost ~on~ *upon* a windowpane.

Newsnotes, I'm Charles Kuralt, CBS News.

*Kuralt often brought his heavy hand to bear on scripts. If he knew that
he could improve the writing, he would do it. If not, he would leave it
alone.*

Teel was not wholly satisfied with the ending, but surrendered it to Kuralt for review. He read it over, took out his black pen and scribbled in eight words at the bottom. It was a new ending and it was perfect: "Now we know ... they didn't even come close."

"It just made all the difference," Teel said. "He didn't use fancy words. It was just this very simple, straightforward, Anglo-Saxon language, but it was the heart of the whole thing."

Teel learned much from Kuralt, and not being one to gush praise, when he told Teel she had done a good job, she knew he meant it. Once, when she showed him a radio piece she had written about bicycles, he exclaimed, "Man, you really worked on this." Teel still feels the tingle from that high accolade.

A revision of the first television piece she wrote also drew Kuralt's commendation. Called "We've Grown Accustomed," the show was a tribute to Americans who died the previous year. "Charles took a look at my first draft, a rather wooden and pedestrian affair and suggested I look for an image to help me," Teel said. "'Like [musician] Harold Arlen's hands on the keyboard,' he suggested. 'Write out,' he said making an expansive gesture from his heart to the world."

Teel worked on the piece all week. When she handed in the script, Kuralt praised her work and ordered her to read it aloud. She began reading timidly—Kuralt stopped her— "No! Read it like you're proud of it," he roared. She bowed to his command. The piece later won an Emmy.

Kuralt made an art of reading aloud. In the early 1980s, he sometimes sat in for Dan Rather on "CBS Evening News." The newsroom was noisy, with Teletype machines clacking out stories, people scrambling all around. But when Kuralt began reading, everyone stopped to listen. "This didn't happen when anybody else was reading the news," Teel said.

Over the years, Teel saw Kuralt do some of his best work. She remembers a particular "Sunday Morning" episode in 1987 called "Footsteps on the Sands of Time,"which played on the same theme as "We've Grown Accustomed." Kuralt choreographed each tribute with a symbol of that person's achievement. For Edward Eppinger, he held up the Daredevil Fishing Lure he had invented. For Fred Astaire, he played a phonograph record. "What most people could not see," Teel said, "was what a wonderful actor Charles was."

Some people also did not appreciate how artful Kuralt was in putting a show like that together so quickly. If he knew he could perform better a second time, he would ask the cameraman, "Do you want it again?" But if he knew he had done the best he could do, he would say, "OK, I think we've got it."

Because he was so sure of himself, "some people thought Charles was lazy," Teel said. "He wasn't. He was just much quicker than everyone else to understand what needed to be done. There wasn't a lot of fussing around. He would come in, do his bit, then say, 'Thank you very much,' and he would walk out of the room, and we would have this thing that was remarkable." "Footsteps" won an Emmy.

Just as Kuralt knew when something could be improved, he also knew when to stop. Teel accompanied Kuralt on a visit to the LBJ Ranch in Texas to interview Lady Bird Johnson about her nationwide beautification project. Kuralt sat down with the former First Lady, composed himself and began to work. Just 20 minutes later, he turned to Teel and said with no hesitation, "All right, we've got it."

"And he knew he had it," she said. "As a producer, I work with a lot of correspondents, and they fish around or just keep talking. But Charles knew what he was after. He was like a fisherman who knew exactly where to throw the hook."

STAGE FRIGHT?

Occasionally, standing before the marquee of stories that opened "Sunday Morning," Kuralt grew woozy. "Every once in a while, he would feel like he wasn't going to get through it," Teel said. "But it would always go away. A second before the lights would go up, he composed his face into the calm, intelligent host that greeted viewers every Sunday morning."

For the first 25 years of his career, Kuralt did his own writing. Then he recruited Peter Freundlich. The two worked together for 14 years, silently most of the time, writing back-to-back.

Back-to-Back Friendship

PETER FREUNDLICH
Writer, "Sunday Morning"

P ETER FREUNDLICH RECEIVED A MESSAGE on his voice mail one day in the early 1980s. It was Kuralt. Odd. Freundlich wrote for CBS Radio Network. He did not usually get messages from Kuralt.

Freundlich spent the better part of a day trying to track him down. "Frankly, I was feeling a little queasy about it," he said. "I thought I was in some sort of trouble."

When Freundlich finally found him, he learned that CBS wanted Kuralt to launch a summer series of "On the Road," five or six stories a week. Freundlich listened, not understanding what it had to do with him. "And I want you to do them with me," Kuralt finally said, "because I can't do them without you."

Freundlich could hardly believe what he had just heard. He remembers nodding dumbly. "I was afraid to actually say to him, 'What do you mean, you can't do it without me?' So I said, 'Yeah, sure,' and walked away."

Freundlich and Kuralt collaborated as writers for the next 14 years. On Sunday mornings, they came to work about 7 a.m. to write leads and finesse scripts for the 9 a.m. broadcast of "Sunday Morning."

Kuralt would amble in and take a seat at his computer. Freundlich would do the same. Then Kuralt would dig out an ashtray from a hollow he had found under the base of his terminal. He was proud of this discovery because it meant his ashtray was always going to be where he could find it, week after week. Freundlich would go off and find a cup to use as an ashtray. "I didn't have the temerity to use his hiding place," he said.

With their cigarettes and their computers before them, the two got right to work. There was no chitchat, no banter about what had to be done. "He was loath to talk about the job, loath to talk about what he needed to do, and I was equally loath to talk about what I was supposed to do," Freundlich said. "Television is full of people who would rather talk about what they do than do it. He just wanted to do it."

Kuralt disdained staff meetings, and the two were always conspicuously absent. "I don't know anybody else who works this way," Freundlich said. "Everybody else has to have meetings, endless meetings. If there was a meeting, Charles would slip out the back."

One of Kuralt's great tricks in later years at CBS was to finagle the use of three offices, making it almost impossible for his bosses to find him. Nobody ever found out how he managed this, but Freundlich thinks it likely that Kuralt never turned in the old keys when he moved from one office to another. "It worked out wonderfully well for his purposes," he said. "Everyone would always assume that if he wasn't in office A, he must be in office B. If he wasn't in office B, you'd assume he was in office C, and then on around the circle. And that's exactly the way he wanted it."

Even in his travels, Kuralt was not one to hang around. "He was smart enough to know that the better you got to know a place and the better you got to know someone, the more of the bad things you would find out," Freundlich said. "Whereas, the first time all you see is the glory of the place and all you get from the person are the best attributes and the best stories. So he would get that, and then he would move on for fear that he would have the bad stuff if he stayed around any longer."

Kuralt sustained his relish for new experiences through-out his life, often telling wonderful stories to his CBS colleagues about the people he had met on the road. "The stories were much better than the people in a lot of cases," said Freundlich, who met a few of the people Kuralt talked about. "Of course, I didn't see them with his enormous enthusiasm."

Kuralt's gift for imbuing his stories about ordinary people and ordinary places with extraordinary value and meaning seemed, to some, suspiciously like folk wisdom. "People less attuned would be ready to say that he was really retelling clichés, because you had the feeling afterward that you had known this all along, but in fact, you had not," Freundlich said. "There was a kind of certainty in the way that he did it that made it sound like folk wisdom, but it wasn't. He had actually noticed it first."

Others like to remember Kuralt's pieces as feel-good, nos-talgic snippets of avuncular Americana, but they were not. "There was a keen poetic intelligence about what he was doing," Freundlich said. "He was so stunned by this country and by this country's people that he was able to make the rest of us see things we wouldn't have been able to see otherwise. And this wasn't patriotism. It wasn't flag-waving. It was a much more interesting and much more complicated love of character and love of the spirit of the place that he spent all his time reporting and writing about."

For the first 25 years or so of his career, Kuralt did his own writing, but over time his profile grew and so did demands on his time. He became too busy to write all of "Sunday Morning." Freundlich, who was initially hired only to help out, began to write more of the show than Kuralt.

In accepting the Silver Baton from Columbia University in 1995 for excellence in television and radio journalism, Kuralt humbly acknowledged Freundlich's role in his winning the prestigious award. "He said he had spent many years appropriating my words and my ideas," Freundlich said. "It was OK with me, because I didn't mind having my words and ideas appropriated by him, because they became enlarged and animated and vivified. That would never have been the case had they not come out of his mouth."

Freundlich saw his colleague rise to the challenge over and over again through the years. The Persian Gulf War began on a Sunday, and suddenly "Sunday Morning," which was the sleepy backwater of CBS, found itself on the front line. "But nothing ever fazed him," Freundlich said. "He was better thinking on his feet. Sometimes it honestly seemed to me as if he didn't need me, or a director, or the camera people. We could have all come back a couple of hours later, and things would have been not only fine, but wonderful."

Eventually, Kuralt became estranged from the industry he built his life around. And he fell out of love with CBS because of budget cuts and layoffs. He resigned in 1994, agreeing to call it retirement because the network chiefs asked him to. Gracious as ever.

Freundlich blames the network for Kuralt leaving. He said CBS finally wore him out. "The company never understood

He started fresh as the network's youngest anchor, but Kuralt's love for the network dimmed in his final years. "It was a long, happy affair, and I was faithful," he wrote in Charles Kuralt's America. *"I loved CBS News ardently at first, as a boy loves a girl. ... My passion tempered as the years went by, but inside the old flame burned. ... Then I woke up one morning and realized I didn't love her anymore."*

that every assignment it gave him was an occasion for anxiety for Charles," Freundlich said. "His standards were so ridiculously high that whatever they wanted him to do had to be done better than anyone else had done it before. They just kept assigning him things to do. Eventually, it got to be too much."

I believe now that the real Charles Kuralt was not the man we lucky few worked with, or sometimes saw away from work. I believe the real Charles Kuralt was the man people saw and heard on the screen. I think that looking for and finding what was best and most true about the rest of us brought out what was best and most true about him.

—Peter Freundlich

I woke up one day and decided I'd done it long enough. But looking back on it, I must say, it was a very satisfying life. There is also this element: I didn't know how to do anything else. I really couldn't have succeeded in the wholesale grocery trade. This was one thing I knew how to do. Of course, as anyone does, I got better at it as I got older. As I look back on it now, I think I'd have done better if I had been a little more relaxed in my life. If I had not pressed quite so hard, if I'd not lost quite so much sleep. I don't think I had a reputation as a hard worker, but inside I was always being eaten up by the pressures. And I think I probably could have done a better job if I had been more mature and been able to take a deep breath and just say, 'Come on. Whether this story gets on the air tonight or not is not really the end of the world. We'll do our best, and that's all we can do.' But I was driven. Not on the surface maybe, but I had a tight stomach all the time. I actually developed ulcers. I don't think I could get an ulcer anymore. I think I've learned better than to put all that internal pressure on myself. I had terrible migraine headaches. The funny thing is, they always came on the rare day when I had a day off. I thought of them as Sunday headaches, because as long as I kept that spring tightly wound, I was fine. When I let it relax, then I suffered, because it was such a change.

—Charles Kuralt, 1996 interview,
Academy of Achievement

I've always talked about resource-fulness, and we came to under-stand that meant study everything and study hard and learn and don't limit what you learn. Whatever comes up, be ready for it. Be able to make use of your intelligence and your learning, to make the world a better place for you, for your family, for everyone else. I think that was what Charles was doing all his life. Anybody could have done those stories and probably done them pretty well. But to copy what he was doing, that was just style. To understand an artist you have to look into his heart, and that's where those stories came from. And that's why people simply could not get a grip on them quite the way Charles did. They didn't have in their hearts quite what he did, the depth of feeling for that story, for that subject.

—Wallace Kuralt in 1998
interview with Ralph Grizzle

I Remember

———

TERRY MARTIN
Executive Producer, "I Remember"

T ERRY MARTIN WORKED WITH KURALT on his last series for
CBS, "I Remember," a CBS News presentation that
focused each episode on a single important event of
the last 30 years. But it was not their first show together. In
the 1980s, Martin was Kuralt's anchor assistant for "America
Tonight."

That show lasted only a year or so, but it produced some
classic Kuralt moments, such as the segment about U.S. sol-
diers spending Thanksgiving in the Persian Gulf. Kuralt did
not have much material to work with. President Bush was in
the Gulf to visit the troops, but the only piece of film Martin
and Kuralt had was of a soldier playing a guitar while the
troops waited for the president to arrive. "Charles looked at it
and said, 'Well, you know, I might be able to do something
with that.' Three hours later," Martin said, "he came down
from his office with this absolutely stunning script about all
the troops who didn't see Bush on Thanksgiving Day. He had

Charles sometimes played down his television pieces as unimportant or fluff. But he really wanted to communicate to us all that there is hope. One man giving one child a bicycle to ride, a child who has never had a bicycle to ride, and teaching him to have the responsibility to take care of the bicycle and bring it back and share it. How in the world can you call that an unimportant act?
—Wallace Kuralt in 1998 interview with Ralph Grizzle.
Above: Jethro Mann, Belmont Abbey's "Bicycle Man"

his own sensibility about this business that was just unique. He was the most consummate craftsman I ever met."

"America Tonight" was broadcast live, even when Kuralt was out of town, and Martin accompanied him on a couple of trips. In the evening, over dinner and drinks, Martin saw a different Kuralt from the sober-sided journalist he worked with on the show.

"He was quite entertaining and extremely knowledgeable and very smart and very charming," Martin said. "The dinners would go for hours, with Kuralt telling stories, enthusiastic about everything. I always had the feeling afterward, at the end of the dinners, that he was kind of sad to see them come to an end."

Martin still saw that same quality when he and Kuralt came back together more than a decade later for "I Remember." "He was getting quite sick at the end, but even when the thing was over with, it wasn't as if he just walked out of the studio and jumped in the car," Martin said. "We'd stand there and talk on the sidewalk for five or 10 minutes. I always had the feeling that he was a very lonely man who really liked companionship but could only take so much of it."

It was hard for Martin to see his friend in decline. As Kuralt became increasingly frail, he seemed to grow sadder, too. While filming "I Remember" in the last months of Kuralt's life, Martin began to feel that Kuralt was giving up.

"That's the memory I will have of him, of his struggling to get into a car because he was so unwell, and feeling that there was more he wanted to say but felt that he had to go."

Following the death of Winston Churchill, Charles and a CBS producer went to the home of Franklin Roosevelt, in Hyde Park, New York, to broadcast a tribute to the late British prime minister. They got there about an hour before the segment was to air. Charles told the producer he wanted a few minutes to wander around by himself. After several minutes, the producer was growing anxious, but Charles stayed calm. He suggested that a camera follow him around Roosevelt's library. He would hold up a book or a letter and talk about them. When the camera started rolling, Charles delivered a long extemporaneous essay on the relationship between England and America and Churchill and Roosevelt. As it happens, Edward Murrow, who was on his deathbed, was watching the broadcast with CBS News President Fred Friendly. Murrow turned to Friendly and said, "That's the best television journalism I've ever seen." That made Charles' place at CBS. It was like a command from Murrow to give Charles a place of dignity at the table, and once given that opportunity, he made the most of it.

—Wallace Kuralt
1998 interview with Ralph Grizzle

Final Episode

MARGERY BAKER
Executive Producer, CBS News

M ARGERY BAKER CHASED DOWN Kuralt after he left CBS in 1994. The network was starting a cable channel that would feature the weekly hour-long series called "I Remember." Baker and others, including Terry Martin, believed nobody could host the series like Kuralt, but it took her three months to convince him.

Kuralt taped two or three episodes at a time, coming to the studio every six weeks. He took scripts that were already written and crafted them to reflect his famous style. "It was very exciting for everyone involved because he had been away from CBS for a couple of years," Baker said. "Whenever he would arrive, a number of people would gather just to chat with him and visit with him. There wasn't any situation where people didn't flock around him and enjoy his company. People glowed in his presence. He brought out the best in everyone.

"That is an unusual trait in our business, to really know that the person you're working with is listening and cares,"

I don't know what I'll be best remembered for doing. I don't think TV reporters of my stature will be remembered. I don't think the world remembers journalists, except the great ones, which I'm not one of. Unfortunately, if you want to be remembered, you have to write. Only the written word survives. One of the sad things about this job is it really doesn't survive. It's gone in a twinkling. It's on the air and never on the air again. It's gone. You can't frame it. You can't send it out to a publisher and hope it sells. It's just a fleeting thing. So I don't think I'll be remembered for anything. And if I do any good, it's just ... you know, the same thing all journalists hope they do. Maybe some good by sort of enlightening people about the times they live in.
                              —August 15, 1965 interview,
                                    The Chapel Hill Weekly.

Photo: Kuralt accepting one
        of his 13 Emmys.

Baker added. "He was a very gentle and kind person, and in many ways delicate. I mean, you knew that with Charles there were borders around him, and he had his private space. And you knew that there were certain places that you didn't step into. And he kept that pretty distinct, and I think most people honored it."

Kuralt taped his last show about five weeks before he died. He told Baker he was not feeling well. He was walking slowly and breathing heavily. He had been to a number of doctors, but none seemed able to identify his condition.

"He looked pale, and for the first time in my memory, he didn't have the same enthusiasm and energy that he had had in the past," Baker said. "It was hard to watch, and it was difficult for him and difficult for all of those of us who were used to working with him in his spirited way."

Still, Kuralt worked as hard as ever, a professional to the end. But when the taping was over, he was exhausted. "It was a very special opportunity," Baker said. "And it was a great privilege for us to have that be his last project, and have it be a project he was very proud of and pleased to participate in."

I have been gone a long time, but now I am home.

—Charles Kuralt,
North Carolina Is My Home.

Homeward
Bound

(The Return To North Carolina, 1994–97)

I N SEPTEMBER 1994, I RECEIVED A PHONE CALL. "Mr. Grizzle,
it's Charles Kuralt. You probably thought I'd died. ..." The
consummate traveler had taken several weeks to answer
the messages I had left for him. At the time, I was a reporter
at a trade magazine for the American Society of Travel Agents.
Kuralt was to be the keynote speaker at the society's annual
conference. My job was to write a profile of him for the
upcoming event.

Kuralt had been "up in Montana doing some fishing." He
sounded jubilant. For close to an hour, we talked about his
career, his North Carolina roots and travel. "Are you a fan of
the West, Ralph?" I told him I was. I said I loved its rugged
beauty.

"It is gorgeous," he rumbled with delight. "I just hold my
breath at the beauty. A couple of days ago, I got going just
about as the sun was coming up. I was coming back from
Billings, back toward western Montana. With the sun behind

me, a cup of McDonald's coffee in the cup holder of the Jeep and the NPR station on the radio, somehow or other everything really seemed right with the world."

This was Charles Kuralt at his best, celebrating simplicity: the Montana landscape, the rising sun, a cup of coffee and the cool-mannered broadcast of National Public Radio. He was in no hurry. He had no hard deadlines. There was no place he had to be. Half an hour into the interview, I asked if he needed to go. "No," he said, and he meant it. "I have all the time in the world right now."

SIX MONTHS EARLIER, Kuralt left CBS. He had grown tired of the "chatter and commotion" of television and the burden of having to answer to an employer. Not that his employer ever knew where he was. He was, of course, on the road for much of his 37 years at CBS.

He thought it unwise to stay too closely in touch with the office. "You get a long line of messages that leaves you no time to do your work the rest of the day," he told the *Greensboro News & Record* in 1994. "You need a little freedom in this life. In this business, you go and go and go. You never have time to think."

Kuralt wanted some time to think. He wanted time to take the days at his own pace, to slow down and be present in life. He told me it all dawned on him at the Winter Olympics in Lillehammer. He was enjoying his time there, but what he really wanted was to hang around in Scandinavia to learn more about the country and the people.

"But no, I had to leave on a certain day and get back to New York to do the 'Sunday Morning' program. And even that much duty, I realized, had become kind of onerous. I longed for an even greater freedom than I had. An inner voice spoke to me and said, 'You have done this long enough, you know that? You're not going to do anything new or better, so you're just going to have to give up your corner office and your big paycheck and strike out and do something different.'"

He returned to New York, and with three years remaining on his contract, he left CBS. Then he set about doing what he loved best—roaming the country with pad and pen. He was going back to where it all started, back to the road.

Kuralt often found refuge at Grandfather Mountain, where good friend Hugh Morton accommodated him in a one-room cabin that looked out on the highest peak in the Blue Ridge Mountains [Mt. Mitchell is the highest peak in the Appalachians] and the valley below. He stayed in the cabin while writing the May chapter of Charles Kuralt's America. *Morton's daughter, Catherine, played the cub reporter, assisting Kuralt with interviews and research. On the last day of his stay, Kuralt rewarded Catherine with breakfast at the cabin. He served up a banquet of grits, eggs, ham, home-baked bread and preserves that someone had given him. It just happened to be Sunday morning, the day when Kuralt would have been standing at the easel for the opening segment of his television time slot. Catherine will always remember that morning as her own private "Sunday Morning with Charles Kuralt."*

An
Explorer's Spirit

CATHERINE MORTON
Friend

AFTER LEAVING CBS, CHARLES KURALT HEADED back to the place he knew best—to his home, North Carolina. He flew into Charlotte on May 5, 1994. Putting nearly four decades of CBS behind him, Kuralt rented a car and drove up Highway 321 through Hickory, turned onto the Blue Ridge Parkway and headed for Grandfather Mountain. "That day was the first day of the rest of his life," said Catherine Morton, who assisted Kuralt while he was researching the May chapter of his sixth and final book, *Charles Kuralt's America.*

Though liberated, Kuralt was anxious about his new beginning. "On the drive up here," he told Morton, "I realized this is the first time in my life I don't have a paycheck to depend on, and I'm a little bit scared."

Over dinner, he explained he had been inspired to leave CBS by basketball great Michael Jordan, who had just walked away from a legendary career to try his hand at baseball.

Kuralt said he felt somewhat the same about television as Jordan finally had about basketball—that he had done everything he had set out to accomplish. "And there were other things left on his list that he wasn't getting around to," Morton said.

"The book, for example. He had the contract to do that book for three years. But he would get rushed. He'd get three days in the town or the place where he wanted to spend the month of May and two days in the place that he wanted to spend the month of June. He wasn't getting to spend the time that he wanted and to immerse himself in the place."

Kuralt also wanted to write an epic poem about Lewis and Clark. And while he never got around to doing that, he did get to pay tribute to an explorer with similar spirit, French botanist André Michaux. Kuralt had discovered, in researching Lewis and Clark, that it was Michaux who first pitched the idea of an expedition to the Pacific Ocean. August 28, 1994, Kuralt arrived at Grandfather Mountain to give the following speech to a crowd of 1,500. It was as close as Kuralt would ever get to the poem he wanted to write.

Two hundred years ago today, a man was climbing Grandfather Mountain. There was no road to the top then, of course, no trail of any kind; and this was his second day of clearing a way through the thick tangles of rhododendron—which mountain people came to refer to as laurel hells—dodging around fallen trees, edging along rock faces, working his way higher. Two hundred years ago tonight, he slept on the ground somewhere up there behind us, and spent another day climbing, and another night impatiently camped, waiting for the break of day. On the fourth day of his ascent, August 30, 1794, he jubilantly recorded in his diary: "Reached the summit of the highest mountain in

North America—I sang the 'Marseillaise' and shouted, 'Long live America and the Republic of France! Long live liberty!'"

He can be forgiven for thinking this old mountain was the highest on the continent. It certainly looks like it might be the highest from down here below. Up on top, it feels like it might be the highest (have you seen Hugh Morton's photograph of the skyline of Charlotte from up there?) and, moreover, in 1794, a higher mountain had not been recorded on this continent in all the annals of exploration.

So here was a 48-year-old Frenchman, standing up there on top of the world, singing to the heavens the new national anthem of his country and shouting to the wind his love for France, and for America, and for the great wave of liberty which had only recently washed across both lands.

His name was André Michaux, and we should all remember his name, for he was one of the most remarkable human beings of the 18th century, or of any century. In paying tribute to his memory here today, we are honoring the great impulses of the human spirit, all of which were in him: courage, vision, strength, generosity, persistence—and intellectual achievement which, in these intellectually lazy times, we can hardly comprehend or appreciate. André Michaux was a linguist—master of French, English, Latin, Greek and every other language he encountered within a few weeks of encountering it, including, in due course, the Cherokee language. He was an explorer, artist, naturalist, scholar. If you asked him what he was, he might have replied, modestly, "botanist." If you ask me, I can only reply, Monsieur Michaux was a piece of work—a man for the ages.

He was a young well-born farmer in France. His beautiful young wife died in childbirth and, in his grief, the farm came to feel like a prison to him. He resolved to escape it by becoming a footloose student of the world beyond his own village. His lively mind and fascination with everything green and growing led him to an association with the great gardeners of the royal gardens at Versailles and at Marie Antoinette's Trianon. Soon, he was making botanical expeditions of his own under the sponsorship of the brother of the king. There was never a horizon beyond which he feared to venture in search of plants and seeds. When it was suggested that he travel east, he traveled east to Baghdad, east to Afghanistan, and on to the borders of India. He was waylaid by bandits and left for dead, naked on a mountain trail in Persia, and while nursing himself back to health, thought he would pass the time by compiling a French-Persian dictionary, and so he did—just one of his incidental accomplishments, a model of linguistic scholarship. When he felt well enough, he returned to France, bringing with him from the east of Europe the camellia and the mimosa, and ginkgo, and pomegranate, and sweet olive and Grecian laurel.

Well, "Thank you, Michaux," said the director of the royal parks and gardens. "And now, will you please go to America and find some useful trees—large ones adaptable to the climate and soil of France for use as timbers for ships?" "Of course," said André Michaux, and within days, he gathered up his 15-year-old son, François, and a trained gardener and a servant, and he sailed for New York. And on arriving in New York, as we say, he hit the ground running. Three weeks later, his first shipment of several boxes was already on its way to France—trees, seeds, cranberries, sweet potatoes. Three weeks after that, he had established a garden on the Hackensack River across the Hudson from New York to produce seedlings and serve as a way station for the plants he discovered in the north. Soon after that, he had established another garden near Charleston, South Carolina, to serve the same purpose for plants he discovered in the South.

In between, he discovered plants—many dozens the world had not known before. He paid his respects to American scholars; he dined with Benjamin Franklin in Philadelphia and George Washington in Williamsburg. But 90 nights of every 100 found him dining sparsely and alone, writing his notes by campfire or under the light of the moon somewhere in the wilderness of the Carolinas or Florida or Georgia, and in those notes, you can read the suppressed excitement of his encounters with live oaks and cypresses, and bay trees and magnolias, and orchids and azaleas.

André Michaux traveled in America for 11 years and along many thousands of miles of Indian trails and animal tracks, often venturing, alone with his pack horses, into territory unknown to settlers. Before he was done, I dare say he knew this country better than anybody else, better than any Indian or woodsman or trapper or trader. Daniel Boone occupies the place in our imagination which really should belong to André Michaux, whose travels were infinitely more daring and more extensive. And unlike Boone and other trailblazers of the period, André Michaux made no claim of land or timber or mineral wealth. The only wealth he sought was scientific knowledge. Seeking it, insatiably, he traveled south into the impassable marshes of southern Florida and north into the tundra of British Canada and west through the thick forests of Kentucky and Illinois and into the unmapped territory west of the Mississippi. He was repeatedly swamped and overturned in flatboats and canoes. His horses wandered away or were stolen. He suffered vile and life-threatening fevers, and hunger and thirst, and bruises and broken bones. His journals hardly mention these hazards and discomforts. His journals say, "Gathered seed," "Prepared seed for shipping," "Shipped 1,168 seeds and plants."

André Michaux went far. He wanted to go farther. In

1793, he proposed to Thomas Jefferson the secret mission that resulted in the journey of Lewis and Clark across the continent to the Pacific Northwest. Loyalty to an undertaking for France is the only thing that prevented Michaux from making that expedition of discovery himself—and 12 years earlier. He wanted to do so, and Jefferson wanted him to do so. Michaux dreamed dreams of waves washing the Pacific Coast, but he never saw them.

He contented himself with returning the next year to the North Carolina mountains, which he now recognized as the great botanical laboratory and paradise of North America. After a few weeks in Charleston that spring, slowly and agonizingly recovering from yet another bout with malaria, he felt strong enough to set out again—up the valleys of Santee and Wateree and Catawba—toward the blue ridges in the distance. It was his first late-summer trip to these mountains, and he found plants new even to him, a new Stewartia between Charlotte and Lincolnton, a lily of the valley on the mountainside above Linville, a flame azalea, white alder and mountain cranberry, the green and growing things that always made his heart beat faster. And in that spirit of excitement, we find André Michaux climbing toward the peak of Grandfather Mountain 200 years ago today. He had been sent to America by the royal establishment of France. But he had lived for nine years now among the formidable democrats of the young American republic, the ones we call the Founding Fathers. And even though he did not know what would become of his own land holdings and possessions at home in the chaos that followed the French Revolution, he had embraced the birth of liberty in France with all his heart, even while nearly starving on one of his wilderness expeditions, refusing a meal from a frontier settler with royalist sympathies who insulted the new French

*Republic. Michaux preferred, as he wrote in his diary, to go
hungry another night and sleep on his deerskin rather than
in the bed of a fanatical partisan of royalty.*

*So now, here he is, a proud citizen of the new France, a
warm friend of the new United States of America, here he is,
200 years ago this afternoon, climbing Grandfather
Mountain. He was alive with the thrill of discovery. He knew
something then that most of us do not appreciate even
today, that this place where he climbed, where we are gathered, is botanically extraordinary almost beyond expressing
it. When André Michaux reached the summit of
Grandfather Mountain, he knew that within his sight on
this mountain and in this summit of Grandfather
Mountain, in a circle of a few miles, exists a greater variety
of plant life than can be found in all of Europe from the arc-
tic capes of Scandinavia to the shores of southern Greece.
Here he found plants and roots which exist—amazingly—
only in the Southern Appalachians, or only here and in
Tibet, or only here and in China. This place was his Eden.
No wonder he stood that day up there at the top of
Grandfather, and shouted in exultation! He would have sung
"The Star-Spangled Banner" but for the inconvenient fact
that it had not been written and would not be for another
20 years.*

*We should all know more of André Michaux. He was a
genuine hero of science and of exploration. His name lives
on, affixed after the Latin names of plants he discovered
among these were 60,000 plants and trees he sent from the
New World to the Old. His great books are there to be read
and learned from, his comprehensive work on American
oaks, and his illustrated two-volume description of growing
things on this continent, Flora Boreali–Americana. His journals are in the care of the American Philosophical Society. I*

Hugh Morton had to coax Kuralt into this friendly encounter with Gerry at Grandfather Mountain's Bear Habitat.

have drawn this brief sketch of his life from the book Lost Heritage, by Henry Savage Jr. And there are other mono-graphs and biographies. To read about his life is to be impressed at every turning of the page.

FEELING FOR THE SWEETNESS

[Kuralt was] talented and lonely, a gentle person who had a remarkable ability to extract the essences of people and situations. He was both bemused by humankind and I think had a feeling for the sweetness of most people.

—Rolfe Neill, friend

Although old friends Charles Kuralt and Hugh Morton were born in the same hospital in coastal Wilmington, they shared a love of the mountains. Kuralt wrote in Charles Kuralt's America *that while he had been born in the flat, eastern part of North Carolina and raised in Charlotte, neither of those places gave him any "particular tingle." But of the Blue Ridge and Appalachian mountains, the sojourner of Grandfather Mountain said, "I feel embraced."*

The Common Touch

HUGH MORTON
Friend

I N THE EARLY 1950s, *COLLIER'S* MAGAZINE COMMISSIONED
Hugh Morton to photograph Charlotte radio broadcaster
Grady Cole, whose homespun wisdom attracted a huge
and loyal following. Such was his charm that the joke ran
that farmers would not get up in the morning until Grady
Cole told them to.

"Cole told me one day the reason I liked to hang around
him was because I'd like some of that common touch,"
Morton said. "I've thought about it many times since, and he
was right. But Charles really had the common touch. He was
so genuine and sincere. I really believe that he was the most
loved, respected and trusted news personality in television."

Morton and Kuralt met in 1960 at the Democratic
National Convention in Los Angeles. Kuralt was there to
cover the convention for CBS. Morton was there as campaign
publicity manager for North Carolina governor Luther
Hodges.

While Kuralt interviewed Hodges, Morton took their picture. Morton and Kuralt struck up a conversation, discovering they both had been born in the same hospital in Wilmington, North Carolina, and had both attended UNC. From that brief conversation, they developed an enduring friendship. In later years, when the traveling reporter could get away, Morton provided refuge at one of the places Kuralt loved best, Grandfather Mountain near Linville, North Carolina. Room and board were cheap, because Morton owned the mountain. It had been passed down to him by his father.

During one visit to Grandfather, the old friends were chatting in the parking lot when a tourist approached. He wanted a picture of his wife with Kuralt. Morton offered to take the photo, so the couple could both be alongside Kuralt. "The fellow thought that was wonderful, but he did not know, as Charles did, that I had been a photographer for 60 years," Morton recalled. "He began an involved and detailed explanation of how to operate the camera. Charles then said, 'Sir, you don't know it, but what you've just done was the same thing as telling van Gogh what to do with the paintbrush.' That was clearly the highest tribute ever paid to my photography."

That was Kuralt's way, Morton said, of poking fun. Always gentle, never mean. He was the same delivering a short speech at Morton's 50th wedding anniversary in Chapel Hill. The crowd was comprised of Chapel Hill and Duke alumni. In his remarks, Kuralt ribbed the Duke bunch by joking that the UNC archrival was necessary because the nation needed a university to send Richard Nixon to study constitutional law.

MORTON WAS NOT SURPRISED when Kuralt died. He had seen Kuralt at Belmont Abbey College a few weeks earlier and was appalled at his weakened condition. "He was just exhausted," Morton said. "I begged him to cancel whatever he had for the coming week and come up here and sleep all day or fish all day or whatever he wanted to do to recover his health. He said he couldn't do it. He had too much to do."

Diagnosed with lupus, Kuralt was being treated with heavy doses of steroids. While on these immuno-suppressants, he succumbed to opportunistic pneumonia and died.

O NE OF MORTON'S FONDEST MEMORIES of Kuralt's gift with words is a speech he gave commemorating the 40th anniversary of the Mile High Swinging Bridge at Grandfather Mountain on September 2, 1992.

Thank you. Nice to be here with so many old friends, and to join in celebrating the birthday of the Mile High Swinging Bridge. When the Mile High Swinging Bridge was completed, opened and dedicated on the afternoon of September 2, 1952, I was starting my sophomore year at Chapel Hill.

There was a great deal of fuss in the newspapers of the state about the Mile High Swinging Bridge, since—as we know—the owner and proprietor of the Mile High Swinging Bridge has never seen any reason to be diffident and retiring about the improvements to his property up here. And from all the stories in the papers, I got the impression that the Mile High Swinging Bridge spanned a chasm one mile deep. You can imagine how I felt when I came up here and saw it for the first time and observed to my surprise that the Mile High Swinging Bridge actually hangs about 80 feet above the ground.

It is calculated that 6 million people have come up here to see the Mile High Swinging Bridge. How many of them would have made the trip if it were advertised as the 80-Foot-High Swinging Bridge? The owner and proprietor of

Charles Kuralt often visited Grandfather Mountain, sometimes to fish, sometimes to write. In 1992, he came to commemorate the 40th anniversary of the Mile High Swinging Bridge. So many people showed up that he had to give his speech twice.

Grandfather Mountain knows what he is doing.

The first winter that the bridge was here, the winter wind came up and blew the bridge around and heaved it like a bedspread being shaken out the back door of the cabin by a mountain woman, and blew a lot of the boards out of the floor, and forced the engineers to give the Mile High Swinging Bridge a second thought. The next spring, they attached those cables that hold the bridge to the ground below. I need hardly point out that since then, the Mile High Swinging Bridge, which is NOT a mile high, is not swinging, either. So what we have here is the 80-Foot-High, Tethered Bridge. Big deal.

And yet, somehow, it IS a big deal, hanging here 5,305 feet above sea level, which gives Hugh Morton a 25-foot margin against any truth-in-advertising lawsuits. If you measure from Wrightsville Beach, it IS a mile high. From the center of the bridge, on a clear day, you can see down into the Linville River Valley 1,600 feet below to the west ... and down into the valley to the east 4,000 feet below.

This is a sufficiently awesome experience to dissuade many otherwise brave men and women from walking across. An extensive survey of 10,000 Grandfather Mountain visitors found that 30 percent of the women, and 12.7 percent of the men come all the way up here and then do not cross the bridge! North Carolina's all-time great athlete, Charlie "Choo-Choo" Justice, who never had the slightest fear of being pounded by 300-pound linebackers, for the longest time could not bring himself to step out on the bridge ... I guess on the theory that while linebackers can drop you to the ground, even they cannot drop you 80 feet to the ground! Charlie Justice has conquered his fear and now strolls across pretending not to be nervous, as do more than 150,000 other visitors every year. The Mile High Swinging Bridge has

*been wonderful for the economy of the mountains. Visitors
stop in neighboring communities to stock up on everything
from picnic supplies to T-shirts, and especially, if they know
they are coming to the bridge, on Dramamine and Valium.*

*No matter how brave you are, if you are a person of nor-
mal imagination, it is impossible to approach the bridge
without wondering if it COULD fall down, and wondering,
IF it could, might it not do so with you in the middle of it.
Visitors would often hold back from stepping onto the bridge
if one or two other people were already on it. Hugh Morton
had an ingenious solution. He put up a sign: Load Limit 40
Persons. He had figured that probably there would never be
more than 40 persons on the bridge at one time, and so 40
persons it became. Actually, the bridge could hold 500 people with no trouble at all. But as soon as that 40 Persons
sign went up, people would count, and if there were only 15
or 20 other people out there, they'd see that it was safe.
That 40 Persons sign did wonders for the traffic on the Mile
High Swinging Bridge.*

*Everybody thinks of the Mile High Swinging Bridge as a
phenomenon of the mountains, but since I am telling you all
the inside stuff this afternoon, you may as well know that it
is actually entirely a product of Greensboro, North Carolina.
It was designed by the architect Charles C. Hartmann Jr. of
Greensboro, by the Truitt Manufacturing Company, and it
was reassembled up here and put in place in three short
weeks by the Craven Steel Erecting Company of Greensboro.
The whole thing cost $15,000, which tells you something
about what has happened to the value of dollars in 40
years.*

*Previous speakers in the history of the Mile High
Swinging Bridge have all been running for something. The
first person to cross the bridge on September 2, 1952, was*

*the Hon. William B. Umstead, who was running for gover-
nor. Candidates will do anything, of course, even risk their
lives. Mr. Umstead lived through it and was duly elected governor two months later. The last time that a formal ceremony was held here was on the fifth anniversary of the bridge,
September 2, 1957, and the speaker that day was another
politician, that great man of North Carolina, United States
Senator Sam J. Ervin Jr.*

*I would just like to say that while this IS an election
year, I am not running for anything, though it appears to me
that everybody else in North Carolina is.*

*No, I am here only to remark on this unique and won-
derful span, and on its owner, a unique and wonderful man.
The bridge is as famous in our beloved mountains as the
Seven Wonders of the World were to the Greeks and Romans
of antiquity. And they probably had anniversary celebrations
like this one to commemorate the Colossus of Rhodes and
the Pharos of Alexandria and the Hanging Gardens of
Babylon. They probably did not have Arthur Smith and
Raymond Fairchild to play the banjo on those occasions ...
though I am not so sure about Arthur. He has been around a
long time and may have been there.*

*I would call the Mile High Swinging Bridge the Eighth
Wonder of the World, except that I went to the Republican
Convention and learned in Houston that the Astrodome is
the Eighth Wonder of the World.*

*But this bridge is the Third Wonder of Avery County, I'll
tell you that ... right after Hugh Morton and Mildred the
Bear ...*

A lot of people ask me what Charles was really like. Of course, I could talk about the man for days and days, but knowing that they wanted a succinct answer, I finally came up with just telling them that I never heard Charles say anything unkind about anybody. That's true, and in thinking about it, it's pretty unusual.

—Loonis McGlohon

North Carolina Was His Home

LOONIS MCGLOHON
Friend

L OONIS MCGLOHON WAS 29 and Charles Kuralt was 16
when they met. A jazz fan, Kuralt came to see
McGlohon, a pianist-composer, rehearse for a weekly
TV show aired on Charlotte's WBT. "He had an infectious
smile and already had a wonderful voice," McGlohon said.
"We went for some coffee and talked about records and
music. Out of that, we became good friends."

In later years, Kuralt would often return to North Carolina
to spend time with McGlohon. Kuralt's favorite escape was to
jump in the car and drive the back roads, which was not
unlike what he did for a living. "He enjoyed visiting places he
had heard of or seen in his childhood," McGlohon said. Places
like Sharon Road in Charlotte, where Kuralt grew up.

McGlohon also traveled to New York to visit Kuralt. What
surprised McGlohon on his visits to the Big Apple was how
easily Kuralt could pass unrecognized. Following a Carnegie
Hall performance by Cleo Laine, Kuralt and McGlohon were

In the early 1980s, North Carolina governor Jim Hunt asked Loonis McGlohon and Kuralt if they would collaborate on some sort of gift to their native state. The result was North Carolina Is My Home.

invited to join Laine and her entourage for a drink at a nearby restaurant. Outside Carnegie Hall, autograph hunters surrounded Laine, but failed to give Kuralt a second look. It was not until the party arrived at the restaurant and Kuralt ordered a drink that heads turned. "The whole place fell silent," McGlohon said. "There was no mistaking that voice."

It always surprised Kuralt that anyone recognized him. "I think he was uncomfortable with his celebrity," McGlohon said. "He never realized he was as well-known as he was."

A few days before his death, Kuralt told McGlohon about a young girl introducing herself in a drugstore. The girl was excited she had just been awarded a Charles Kuralt scholarship. "He was very impressed that this girl would recognize him and that she should be the recipient of a scholarship named for him," McGlohon said. "He was just a very happy pup to tell that story."

Despite his celebrity, Kuralt maintained his down-home charm. "I have seen him in situations that might have been a little tedious and banal," McGlohon said. "He would be busy and get stopped on the street by a couple of farmers who were in town for the day, and they would tell Charles about their corn crop. He would listen with great interest. He never tried to get away from the conversation, and in fact, 10 or 15 minutes later he would say to me, 'I never knew that about Silver Queen corn.'"

The two friends also performed together on stage, presenting "North Carolina Is My Home" to audiences up and down the East Coast. One of the last concerts the two performed together was with the Charlotte Symphony shortly before Kuralt died. McGlohon knew then that something was wrong. "Backstage he was stretched out on a sofa, just exhausted," McGlohon said. "But he walked on that stage, and he reached down and pulled up that reserve of energy.

Kuralt and McGlohon performed North Carolina Is My Home *for audiences some 50 times.*

You would never have thought he felt bad until it was over, and then the energy level was gone."

By McGlohon's measure, Kuralt was a borderline hypochondriac. He did not like visiting the doctor's office for fear he would find out something was wrong. "The day after the concert, before he went back to New York for the last time, he told me and my wife: 'You know, I'm bleeding in my mouth a lot. It's not my throat. I don't know where it's coming from.' My wife told him to call an orthodontist as soon as he got back to New York. 'You've probably got some gum problems.'"

Of course, it was not gum problems. It was lupus.

"I don't think Charles was in great physical shape for the last 20 years," McGlohon said. "He smoked too heavily, and his diet wasn't good. He didn't exercise much, and in the last two or three years it was difficult for him to walk more than a half mile without being winded, really winded."

McGlohon tried to talk to Kuralt about smoking, but it became a sore point. He finally told McGlohon: "Listen, that's the one thing I've got left. Let me enjoy that."

The night before he died, Kuralt told McGlohon he was getting out of the hospital. He had work to do for CBS but was concerned, because his face was blotchy. "I don't think he had any premonition that the end was that near. He talked about the hospital food being so bad. He said he sure would love to have a good hamburger. When we hung up, he said, 'I love you, buddy.' And that was the last time we spoke."

When Bob Timberlake asked Kuralt why he had agreed to collaborate on
The Bob Timberlake Collection, *Kuralt told him, "Well, this business
I'm in really is kind of fleeting, and there are some things that I want to
say, things that I want to put down in print, something that will last."*

Homespun

—

BOB TIMBERLAKE
Friend

T WO OF NORTH CAROLINA'S FAVORITE SONS, Bob Timberlake and Charles Kuralt collaborated in 1977 on a limited-edition book, *The Bob Timberlake Collection.* Kuralt provided the text to accompany 75 of Timberlake's paintings—Kuralt drew inspiration from his boyhood in rural North Carolina. "I remember his coming to my log cabin and pulling a manuscript out of a manila envelope," Timberlake said of Kuralt's draft. "There were six or seven of us standing around, and someone had the presence of mind to ask Charlie to read it to us. By the time he was done, there wasn't a dry eye in the crowd." Following is an excerpt from that draft.

Here, come and sit, just here beside me for a while, my daughter. There are some things I have forgotten to tell you ...

... what happened is this: I met a painter, also a North Carolinian, who, like me, had known some of these old things himself, and heard tell of many others, and has felt

They had many wonderful conversations, but Bob Timberlake remembers his July 1, 1997, phone call with Kuralt as the worst in his life. Kuralt was in a New York hospital. "I asked him what in the world he was doing in the hospital," Timberlake said. Kuralt replied he was really "bad off" and "tired of this mess." "The doctors don't know what's wrong with me," Kuralt said. "All I want them to do is leave me alone and let me go to sleep." Timberlake was distraught about what he thought Kuralt was implying by wanting to go to sleep. "Well maybe I can come get you, and we can go back to North Carolina and get some good barbecue and go trout fishing up with Hugh Morton," Timberlake said. But Kuralt said, "No, I'm past all that. I just want to go to sleep."

within himself the strong urge to get it down, as much as he can, and pass it on.

His paintings have reminded me of the homely beauty of ordinary things, of the careless perfection of nature, of the richness of human talk and song, the value of friendship and neighborliness. His urge became my urge. These are fragments of stored memories.

... the people who lived in the old houses were more grateful to God than we are. I am sure of that, and I think I know a reason: They knew His work better than we do. They knew the uses of everything that grows.

They knew that a sassafras root, if boiled, makes a fine kettle of tea, and if boiled longer, makes a pretty orange dye for a bolt of homespun or a cotton dress.

They knew that the youngest leaves of the poke plant, gathered in the spring while they are tender, and washed and boiled and seasoned with salt and bacon, made a salad ... they knew God's gifts. In the autumn leaves, or in the sunsets, we sometimes appreciate His vivid colors. They wore them on their backs.

... our existence is in the past, as well as in the future. Unless we know very well where we have been, we cannot see where we are going. That is why I wanted you to have these glimpses of simple verity and unselfconscious—because they are growing rarer as we rush to pave the forests and subdivide the meadows and find substitutes for natural things. Those old houses and the people who lived, and still live, in them have something of value to tell us, something satisfying to show us.

We say that truth and beauty cannot be substituted for, that they are eternal. But if we never listen to the quiet, knowledgeable voices of the past, which of us can ever distinguish between the truth and shallow illusion ...

I always feel like a North Carolina boy a long way from home when I'm in Thailand or Zaire.

—Charles Kuralt in 1994 interview with Ralph Grizzle

'Scuse Me, Ain't You Mr. Kuralt?

JANE KISER
Friend

KURALT SPENT MARCH OF 1995 in Charleston, South Carolina, gathering material for his book *Charles Kuralt's America*. His companion for that month was Jane Kiser, a Charleston tour operator he hired to show him around.

One afternoon, Kuralt and Kiser were lunching at a downtown restaurant catering predominantly to African Americans. A customer, an elderly lady, walked over to Kuralt's table and said, "'Scuse me, ain't you Mr. Kuralt?" He stood up and bowed. "Yes, ma'am, and who are you?" Then, in the same breath, he urged the newcomer to make the lunch a threesome.

It was classic Kuralt, charming and personable, delighted to make a new acquaintance. The old lady took a seat, and Kiser watched as Kuralt "very skillfully picked the entire story of the old woman's life." He asked about segregation and about stories the woman had heard from her mother.

Kuralt was guest of honor at a cocktail party hosted by a friend of Jane Kiser, his Charleston guide. He noticed one of his books propping up one corner of a sofa. "It's good to know that I'm still serving," Kuralt quipped. The host was red-faced, but it was good for a laugh, Kiser recalled.

"By the time she got ready to leave, he was her dearest friend."

As she was leaving, the old lady stood up, put her arms around Kuralt and said, "Welcome to Charleston."

"It was wonderful to watch," Kiser said. "And he was truly interested in what she had to say. I think Gabriel could have blown his horn and Kuralt wouldn't have blinked an eye, because he was listening so intently to her."

Kiser saw Kuralt's skill with people as "a God-given talent," something that couldn't be faked. "He had the ability to make anybody, whether it were a king or a pauper, feel instantly at ease, to open up, to confide in him, as though he were their best friend. The world is filled with people who know how to stand in front of a camera and talk, but not everybody has the ability to make you feel you're really somebody special."

But for all his ability to lay people open, Kiser sensed there was a lot of "hidden Charles there, a façade perhaps." She was not suggesting he was anything less than genuine in his interest, but she wondered how much more lay beneath Kuralt's own skin.

There certainly was a private personality behind the one viewers saw on television. For example, Kuralt confided in Kiser that he was an agnostic, which she found hard to believe, because he questioned everything at great length. "As we all get ready to meet our maker, even if you don't believe in one, I think we try to find the purpose of life," Kiser said.

There is little doubt that Kuralt was looking for something in his final years. In the foreword to *Charles Kuralt's America*, he wrote that shortly before leaving CBS, "a desire for substance and reality came over me."

"He seemed to be a very uncomplicated person on the surface, but I think that there was a void there," Kiser said. "There was loneliness there."

Kuralt told Kiser he had regrets, one being he wished he had spent more time raising his children. "I guess if you're going to be successful, there's a price tag that goes with it, and looking back, maybe he regretted the price he paid."

His own father died shortly before Kuralt came to Charleston, and he was still grieving. When he talked with Kiser about his childhood, she saw a lot of pain. "I think he tried to live up to his father's expectations. His father was so important to him that he was driven to fulfill his father's dreams. Maybe they started out as his father's and became his, but I really got the feeling that he was living his father's life for a good portion of it."

After spending every day for nearly a month with Kuralt, Kiser began to see hints of impatience, particularly with certain types of people. They attended a cocktail party where "everyone was trying to be a blueblood and outdo the others with their pompous ways." Kuralt was polite and gracious through the evening, but when he and Kiser left, she asked what he thought of them. "Total jerks," he replied.

When he first contacted Kiser about the Charleston trip, Kuralt told her not to bother making appointments with the hierarchy. He wanted to meet common, everyday people. Kuralt had a penchant for recording history from the bottom up, through interviewing average, unfamous people rather than through presidents and celebrities.

In fact, Kiser sensed that Kuralt could be intolerant with with people who weren't "real." "With people who appeared false or pretentious, he did not want to be bothered," Kiser said. "But with old people, children or folks who were not well-educated, he had infinite patience."

Maybe what he saw in those people was a certain beauty. Kiser said Kuralt had a keen appreciation of beauty, especially the daffodils that were blooming at the time. He bought them fresh at the grocery store every morning. For her birthday, Kuralt gave Kiser a pot of red tulips. "He was a terribly romantic man—I mean romantic from the standpoint of remembering the little niceties that make life better," she said. "The red tulips, I cherish because I don't like cut flowers, they die too quickly, so this was something that lived on even after he left."

A day after Kuralt's memorial service in Chapel Hill, Bill Friday heard from a man in central North Carolina. "You don't know me," the man said, "but I have kept up with what you and Charles have done, and I want to give the headstone for his grave." The offer was accepted. "The powerfulness of Charles' life and the example he set brought forth acts of grace that I don't think anybody would have even thought about but for him," Friday said.

Final Letter

BILL FRIDAY
Friend

BILL FRIDAY, PRESIDENT EMERITUS OF UNC, was Kuralt's dean when Kuralt was the editor of *The Daily Tar Heel*. And in the years that followed, it was not uncommon for Friday to hear from him out of the blue. One of those calls came on a Saturday afternoon. Kuralt was working on his lead-in for "Sunday Morning."

"Tell me what to say about intercollegiate sports," Kuralt said. "Give me a lead story."

"We talked for 30 or 40 minutes," Friday said. "That's the way it was. He'd be anywhere and everywhere and all of a sudden he'd call. He'd say, 'Well I just called to see if the dogwoods are blooming and if the flowers are up.' He was homesick. This was where his soul stayed."

On July 4, 1997, Friday's phone rang at 6 a.m. Kuralt's assistant, Karen Beckers, was on the line. "The minute she identified herself, I knew something was wrong," Friday said. "And she said, 'I've called you because I must tell you that

Dear Bill,

Thanks for your note. I have been in the
hospital, groggy and a good deal out of it.
I don't think I am dying; in fact, I seem
to be recovering nicely; but this experience
has given me intimations of mortality. I
know you have better things to worry about,
but I thought I would ask if you have any
way of finding out if there are a couple of
burial plots in Chapel Hill? Of course, the
campus would be ideal, but I know that is
probably out of the question. Maybe over
the next week or two you could have somebody
inquire about availabilities in town. And
if that is also out of the question I will
go farther afield. I should have thought of
this forty years ago! Sorry to ask you to
look into such a bizarre question.

Love to Ida. And I hope to see you before
the roses finish blooming.

As ever,

Charles

July 2, 1997

*I am only now beginning to appreciate
the love I have for Chapel Hill. It
is a moving place. The more I think
about it. And you have made it
so. C.*

Kuralt's letter requesting that his final resting place be in Chapel Hill.

Charles is gone.'"

Friday was devastated. Beckers told him she had talked to Kuralt at 7:30 p.m. the day before to remind him that a baseball game was on television. Kuralt said to her: "My fever's out of control. I'm having terrible spasms, and something has gone bad wrong." By 4 a.m. he was gone.

Beckers also told Friday that Kuralt had sent him a letter the day before. In it, he asked if Friday could find him a place to be buried in Chapel Hill. Friday had not yet received the letter, but, of course, he would oblige.

"I called the city manager, Cal Horton, and told him what I was up against," Friday said. Horton met Friday at the Old Chapel Hill Cemetery on the UNC campus. They studied a map of the cemetery that Horton had brought along and discovered that Chapel Hill resident George Hogan had several plots. They called Hogan. He said, "No, I won't sell them." Horton and Friday waited in anticipation of Hogan's explanation. "But I'll give Charles two."

Hogan worked for the Educational Foundation at UNC when Kuralt was editor of *The Daily Tar Heel*. "He used to irritate me a little bit," Hogan recalled. "He was a liberal back in those days, and he didn't think athletes should get scholarships." But in later years, Hogan remembered Kuralt as the "only man I could watch on television without turning it off." Thus the reason he donated the two plots.

Kuralt's public was just beginning to pay homage. Later, a brown cardboard box arrived at Bill Friday's office. It was from Granville Hall, a horticulturist in Virginia who Kuralt had interviewed a couple of times on CBS. Hall had named a new jonquil for Kuralt—there were 100 of the bulbs in the box. "We're now placing all of these in a design on Charles' grave," Friday said during our interview, "so that next spring the jonquils will rise again."

Care about one another, and not only those of your own clan or class or color. I wish you long life and good fortune, of course. But my warmest wish for you is that you be sensitive enough to feel supreme tenderness toward others, and that you be strong enough to show it. That is a commandment, by the way, and not from me. I believe it is also the highest expression of civilization.

—Charles Kuralt
Commencement
UNC-Chapel Hill
May 12, 1985

Remembering

W E REMEMBER CHARLES KURALT IN MANY WAYS. I remember him for presenting me with people to admire and for teaching me that heroes often are found not on the main roads of life but on the less-traveled back roads. He showed them to be people living in our own towns, perhaps just next door, like the retired North Carolina minister who spent his golden years repairing bicycles for the poor black kids in his community, or the Mississippi share-cropper who somehow managed to send eight children to college. Kuralt presented us with a refreshing definition of heroes—just ordinary people doing extraordinary things.

Visiting the hamlets along America's back roads gave Kuralt a great deal to be reassured about. In return, he reas-sured us. Through him, we became acquainted with Americans who were "decent and compassionate and unsul-lied by arrogance or hostility toward other people" as Kuralt described them. They were driven not by "motives of greed" or "delusions of superiority," but by genuine concern for their communities and their country. Their only motives were to help make America a better place to live. "It's what we used to call 'patriotism,' before that became such an old-fashioned word," Kuralt said.

One of Kuralt's people was Montana native Gordon Bushnell. "Mr. Bushnell always thought there ought to be a straight highway from Duluth to Fargo, and the state would not build it," Kuralt told me. "So he decided that he was just going to have to build it himself."

All alone, with a No. 2 shovel, an old wheelbarrow and an ancient John Deere tractor, Bushnell began negotiating with people for the right to build a road across their land. "When we met him, he had finished 11 miles of road, had 180 miles to go—of course, he was 78 years old at the time," Kuralt recalled with a laugh. "But I loved him, and he just pressed on, because he knew it was the right thing to do."

Despite the cynicism of the time, Kuralt believed Americans had an inherent sense of the right thing to do, and he loved them for it. Kuralt's America was one of good and decent people. He inspired me, as I am sure he inspired many others, with his entertaining stories of goodness.

He told us that maybe, just maybe, we were all better off than we thought we were. In 1993, Kuralt sat on an airplane next to a college graduate, listening to him complain about job prospects. The new grad believed it must be the worst time in history to be looking for a job. Kuralt silently recalled how his father, fresh out of college in the 1930s, set out to look for a job, and after six months of searching, found one: creosoting telephone poles in eastern North Carolina. "I didn't say anything to the young graduate," Kuralt said, "but I thought, Didn't they teach you any history in that great university of yours?"

Kuralt's America was one of self-reliant, self-determined, problem-solving people. National conscience was more than a concept to him. It was something real, "a naive idea," he said, "but one that we really believe in," and one that we cannot shake.

"The idea we adhere to is a very appealing one to me," he said. "It is that there is a solution to every problem. Let something go wrong in America, and you can be sure somebody will form a committee. Next thing you know, people are at work on the problem just as if there really were a solution to it. It's the most appealing thing of all to me about our fellow citizens."

In his lifetime, various "handfuls of people, willing to be ridiculed," stood up for what they believed. Through their perseverance, he added, they succeeded in raising awareness of our environment, women's rights, racial inequality and other national concerns. "It still amazes me that even in this big, complex society, one man or one woman can make all the difference."

His words were reassuring; his presence, comforting. He saw the best of who we were. "The country that I have found does not bear much resemblance to the one we read about on the front pages of newspapers or hear about on the evening news," Kuralt said. "The country that I found presents cups of coffee and slices of apple pie and people who always want you to stay longer than you have time to."

I know how those people feel. I thought Charles Kuralt would stay forever. I wish he had stayed longer.

I'd like to write something that would live. It's getting a little late. I'd better get at it if I'm going to do that. In television, everything is gone with the speed of light, literally. It is no field for anybody with intimations of immortality, because your stuff, by and large, doesn't live on. It's not easy for me to admit, but I would love to write something that people would still read 50 or 100 years from now. That comes with growing older. You begin to think, 'Well, what have I ever done to benefit society? What have I ever written that would excite a young reader years from now, the way Mark Twain's journalism still excited me when I first read Roughing It *and* The Innocents Abroad?' *So we can't all be Mark Twain. In fact, I guess it's fair to say, none of us can be Mark Twain, except Mark Twain. But you do begin to yearn to write something that gains a little permanence.*

—Charles Kuralt, 1996 interview
Academy of Achievement

Farewell, my friends. Farewell and hail.
I'm off to seek the Holy Grail.
I cannot tell you why.
Remember, please, when I am gone
'Twas aspiration led me on.
Tiddly-widdly-toodle-oo.
All I want is to stay with you.
But, here I go. Goodbye.

—Charles Kuralt's parting words on
"Sunday Morning," April 3, 1994

In memory of
Charles Bishop Kuralt
1934–97